Contents

Introduction.   What is an official publication?

The answer to this at one level is quite simple – it is a publication issued by or for a governmental body and is also known as a 'government publication' or 'government document' – but at another level it is far from simple and librarians have argued over what should be included or excluded for many years. Even the definition of IFLA (the International Federation of Library Associations and Institutions) of 1983 has not settled the matter (see Appendix).

In general there is not much dispute about what constitutes a 'publication'. It is any printed book, paper or periodical (or any microform, electronic or other surrogate for the same), offered for sale to the public or issued to them at no charge. Thus, obviously, unique manuscripts and typescripts duplicated in small quantities for internal use are not 'published'. Neither are printed documents that remain unissued to the public, that are confidential or classified, or simply – without being particularly secret – are not made generally available to the public. However, there is a major exception to the last category. Inter-governmental organisations or IGOs (see below) generally issue their publications in two categories: 'publications' so-called, or 'sales publications' which are conventionally printed, priced and put on sale to the public and 'documents', which are often reproduced from typescripts, unpriced and normally free. These are produced in small print runs primarily for participants in the activity concerned and distributed to depository collections, with a few copies spare for those who want them. These too are considered to be publications for the purposes of defining official publications and, indeed, constitute the main output of IGOs.

What constitutes 'official' is less easy to define succinctly. It obviously includes the output of the governments of nation states and, in the case of federal states, those of both federal governments and the constituent governments of its states or provinces. It also includes the governments or administrations of local authorities within states at every level – regional, county, district, municipal or parish (though local government publications will not be considered in this work) – for a government does not have to be a *sovereign* government. For the same reason, it includes the publications of devolved governments and the governments of dependent territories, now just a dwindling collection of tiny territories but once comprising most of Asia and Africa and, earlier still, the Americas and Australasia as well. Finally it includes inter-governmental organisations (IGOs). International organisations are of two types – those whose membership is comprised of the governments of nation states (IGOs) and those whose membership is comprised of organisations (other than governments) or individuals from various countries (NGOs – international non-governmental organisations). Thus obviously the UN is an IGO but so are OECD, NATO and the European Union but IFLA, whose members are library associations, libraries and librarians from many countries, is an NGO.

All the outputs of IGOs are official but what constitutes 'governments' of territories and therefore what outputs are official, is less clear. The traditional constitutional theory is that 'government' has three arms – the executive, the legislature and the judiciary. The judiciary, the system of courts of law, the judges and officers of the courts, issue few publications but such as they do are all official. Law reports, widespread in common law countries such as England or the United States, are issued by and for the legal profession and are not reckoned as official.

The legislature, the principal law-making body of the state and, usually, the organ that holds the executive to account, has a much more extensive output. Firstly, there is legislation, though this is often considered to be the output of the state as a whole, but, either way, it is obviously official. Then there are the records of its debates, the minutes, agenda papers and other records of the proceedings, and finally, there are a wide range of information papers that it needs to be properly informed in carrying out its tasks. All these are official.

It is the executive that is hardest to define. Firstly it is a small group of politicians that collectively take the major policy decisions about running the country. Individually they are called ministers (though their offices have various designations) and collectively they used to be known in Britain as 'the Ministry' but this term has now become old-fashioned and '*the* Government' (as in 'The Government decided …') is the modern term. Below this level are the various government departments and ministries and their component branches, departments and units. It is the output of these that constitutes the bulk of official publications emanating from the executive.

But as the scope of government has increased in modern times, so the procedures of administration have become more diffuse. Several examples will suffice. Until the nineteenth century the provision of education was a private matter. Then, with small beginnings (modest government subsidies to educational charities) the state became increasingly involved and now funds, through subventions from national government, and runs, through local education authorities (LEAs), the full range of primary and secondary education. Provision is made through schools and other educational establishments. In the same way the provision of the health services has largely been annexed by the state. In both cases, state provision is paralleled by a small but vigorous private sector. There is a strong state involvement in the provision of culture; some institutions were founded by the state (most of the national museums) and many more are largely funded by grants from government and some are run by government (mostly local government in this area). In Britain and in many other countries, the tendency is to regard the publications emanating from the providers of these services, the schools and colleges, the hospitals and clinics, the libraries, museums and galleries, as not being official publications. The output of the bodies administering the providers, the LEAs, the NHS and the government departments is, however, regarded as governmental.

For much of the twentieth century a growing quantity of industrial and commercial concerns had been taken over by the state and not just in centrally-planned economies (the communist countries and their largely third-world imitators). In Britain, postal services were provided by the state from the seventeenth century and in the nineteenth century a growing number of public utilities were municipally run, mostly gas and electricity undertakings but also things like tramways and harbours. In the mid-twentieth century the gas and electricity undertakings, both municipal and private, were nationalised as were the coal industry, much of public transport (especially the railways) and the steel industry. Other businesses in public ownership included the telephone services, national airlines, certain ports and airports, broadcasting, the nuclear industry and a few enterprises hard to categorise such as Thomas Cook, the travel agents, or the Carlisle pubs. In none of these cases were the publications of the enterprises themselves considered official except for the Post Office, including the telephone service, which was directly administered by a government department with the Postmasters-General responsible for it in Parliament. Many, however, had a statutory requirement to render an annual account of themselves to Parliament and the Report and accounts (later just their financial accounts) were and are considered official. In the late twentieth century the tendency to take major enterprises into public ownership has been put into sharp reverse world-wide but nowhere more so than in Britain. This is obviously important both socially and economically (whether for good or ill) but, from the point of view of defining what is an official publication, it is, at least in Britain, of little consequence, as the publications of such bodies are not generally considered official whether the bodies themselves are in public ownership or not.

Another example of the diffusion of government needs to be considered. There has been an increasing trend for certain activities formerly directly undertaken by civil servants in government departments now to be undertaken by executive agencies hived off from the parent ministry and operated at arm's length. Thus, formerly, in the days of the Ministry of Pensions and National Insurance, payment of unemployment and other benefits and old age pensions was made through local offices of the Ministry; now all this is handled, largely remotely, by the Benefits Agency and by some more specialised agencies such as the Child Benefit Agency and the War Pensions Agency. Most government departments have spawned a range of such agencies, part of the department but autonomous. Some departments have resisted. The local tax offices of the Treasury (Inland Revenue) are directly administered by the Treasury and are not part of a Tax Agency though there are agencies associated with the Treasury – National Savings, the Office for National Statistics (ONS) and the Royal Mint are all Treasury executive agencies.

Many other public bodies exist exercising governmental functions or funded by or answerable to government: regulatory bodies (many established to regulate denationalised commercial monopolies), advisory bodies, funding bodies, commissions, authorities, research councils, laboratories and so on. The following, taken at random, will give a flavour of the range of such bodies – ACAS, the National Physical Laboratory, the College of Arms, the Royal Fine Arts Commission, the Audit Commission, the Strategic Rail Authority, the British Standards Institution, the Broads Authority, the Countryside Agency, the Crown Estate, the Design Council, English Nature, the Equal Opportunities Commission, the Government Hospitality Fund, the Housing Corporation, the Intelligence Services Tribunal, the Land Registry, the Corporation of Trinity House, the Medical Research Council, the Ordnance Survey, the Office of the Parliamentary Commissioner (the Ombudsman), the Parole Board for England and Wales, Ofsted, the Wales Tourist Board, Companies House and the UK Sports Council. With institutions as varied as these, consistency is difficult to achieve; some publish little anyway but others are major publishers and in general their output is considered official especially if it is issued in connexion with a function formerly undertaken more directly by the government.

In some countries the definition of an official publication is considerably wider. It would include many of the categories excluded above and include others such as the publications of central banks and political parties (especially in one-party states). For this reason, IFLA in its definition (see Appendix) was unable to secure a single universally acceptable definition and had to give the widest possible definition and qualify the peripheral categories as being official in any country if so regarded in that country. In Britain, for the most part, publications of institutions identified in notes (2), (3) and (4) of that definition are not considered official. But even with a more restricted definition, the numbers are vast. The British Library's collection of official publications occupy some 45 km of shelves. Most of the documents are not individually catalogued and it is difficult to estimate realistically how many separate items this represents – perhaps 25 million. But this does not exhaust the Library's holdings of such material; there are substantial holdings of official publications elsewhere in the Library, in its Science, Technology and Business Collections (including a vast collection of patents), in the Oriental and India Office Collections, in the Map Library, scattered among the general collections of the Library, especially in the stock of older material and in the collections of the Document Supply Centre. In all, this may increase the Library's holdings of official publications by perhaps a third and official publications may well account for one in five or more of the British Library's total stock.

In a monograph as brief as this, it would be quite impossible to cover at any worthwhile level all official publishing and this work has a much more limited aim. It concentrates first of all on British official publications and within that on the more important categories – legislation, parliamentary proceedings and papers, and mainstream departmental publications. There follows a chapter on some specialised cases to exemplify the range of official publications and chosen because they are frequently requested in the British Library. The chapters on foreign official publications and those of IGOs are not so much selective as simply showing a few examples of what exists. In all cases, the nature of the publications are explained in some detail as this is the key to understanding how to find them. The last chapter is devoted to electronic sources, both bibliographic sources to identify publications and sources for the texts themselves. It consists largely of a list of CD-ROMs and online sources. It might seem that apparently 'relegating' this information to a final chapter is an indication that electronic sources should be considered an afterthought for finding official publications. On the contrary, they are often already the first source one should use and their importance will only grow. In a sense, however, they are too large a topic for a work of this compass and deserve a separate monograph all to themselves. Also, developments in this area are frighteningly rapid and any information provided is likely soon to become out of date whereas the rest of the work should have a reasonable shelf-life (though it may well be superseded by a better work).

It is obvious, therefore, that this work omits as much or more than it contains but it should be only a starting point for your research. Although public libraries usually have larger collections of official publications (especially legislation and *Hansard*) than they are often given credit for, most people seeking official publications will use major research libraries for that purpose. These will usually have substantial holdings of such material organised as a discrete collection and with specialist staff to look after them and to assist readers. *Use this staff.* You, and only you, can do your own research but how you do it and where you find what you want or, better still, what you *need* is another matter. That is what guides like this are for, but printed or electronic information sources may not formulate your problem as you see it and therefore the solution may not fit your perceived need. You can discuss all this with the specialist staff at the research library where you are working. A five-minute discussion with an expert may save you hours of fruitless and frustrating searching among printed or electronic sources. Then you can come back to those sources, though this time with a reformulated search strategy.

Chapter 1. Laws and how to find them

The principal function of any government of an organised state is to maintain peace and stability in the country. This is done by organising the defence of the country against external aggression and by preserving law and order within it. The former function generates little in the way of publications but the latter requires that the laws necessary to maintain order are known to its citizens who have to obey them. In the earliest days before printing this was done by requiring local officials such as the sheriffs in each shire to proclaim the laws to gatherings of local citizenry. Even now proclamations are still used for certain administrative functions such as the dissolution of Parliament and the calling of a fresh general election, though in published rather than declamatory form.

Soon after its introduction, printing was adopted as the principal means of promulgating official and definitive texts of laws. In 1484 the acts of parliament of Richard III's only Parliament were published in a slim volume that marks the small start of official publishing in England. Since then, at the end of each parliamentary session, all the statutes or acts of parliament of that session have been published in a volume per session until 1939, after which the volumes have been annual (calendar year) rather than sessional. Parliament was not obliged to meet each year until 1689 and did not do so. For this reason the sessional volumes of statutes were at first irregular but, with this proviso, the series of volumes of acts of parliament, begun well over five hundred years ago, constitutes the longest running serial publication of all.

That first printed volume of acts of parliament was the start of official publishing in this country in another sense. The printer of the volume, one W. Machlinia according to the Latin imprint (presumably from Mechelen or Malines in the Low Countries), was granted by letters patent the monopoly of printing acts of parliament. Such patents have continued to be issued down to the present and the Controller of Her Majesty's Stationery Office is also the Queen's Printer of Acts of Parliament. This, in fact, is the only instance of an official 'government printer' in Britain. HMSO had long been a major (*the* major) publisher of British official publications and since privatisation The Stationery Office Ltd (TSO) has continued to be. Neither publisher however, had or has a monopoly of government publishing except for the patent for acts of parliament which was retained by the residual HMSO when the bulk of its activities were privatised as TSO.

Once the contemporary publishing of sessional volumes of statutes had been established, other developments followed, notably the retrospective printing of statutes that predated printing and the issue of cumulative editions of acts of parliament. Earlier statutes were first published in two volumes called *Nova statuta* (1505) and *Vetera statuta* (1508), New statutes and Old statutes where 'new' was defined as from 1327 onwards, the start of the reign of Edward III. Conventionally statutes go back to 1215, the date of *Magna Carta*, although the earliest statute is reckoned as the *Statute of Merton* of 1235 and the earliest still in force is the *Statute of Marlborough* of 1267 (now renamed the *Distress act 1267* (52 Hen 3, cap.1)). In fact *Magna Carta* is on the statute book but 'statutory' *Magna Carta* is rather different from the historical document signed (or rather sealed) by King John at Runnymede in 1215. This was repudiated within months and a new *Magna Carta* was issued shorn of the provisions most restrictive of royal power. It was reissued with further modifications ten years later in 1225 in the name of Henry III (whose personal rule dates only from 1227). This was confirmed at regular intervals and it is Edward I's confirmation of Henry III's 1225 reissue of *Magna Carta* that is the *Magna Carta* of the statute book – *Confirmation of liberties act 1297, etc.* (25 Edw.1 cap.1, 9, 29 & 37).

Statutes at large of 1587 was not the first cumulative edition of the statutes but it was the first of a series of this name that continued to be issued through the seventeenth and eighteenth century under the same title. 'At large' signified that it contained no summaries or abridgements but it did not mean that all acts were included. Short-lived acts (including most 'tax' acts which last only for 12 months) and those of a local character were omitted, as were all private acts. These were identified as a separate series in 1539 and they were entirely unpublished although they were numbered and listed in the King's/Queen's Printer's edition of sessional volumes of acts and they were also listed in *Statutes at large*. The definitive version of this was the 1762–65 edition by Owen Ruffhead (*Statutes at large* are often referred to as 'Ruffhead') and later editions down to the end of the eighteenth century and beyond were essentially continuations of this.

For acts of parliament up to the end of the reign of Queen Anne (up to 1713, to be precise) the definitive text is to be found in an edition called *Statutes of the realm*. This was issued by the Record Commissioners, the forerunners of the Public Record Office (now part of The National Archives) who compared all the extant manuscripts as well as the printed editions to date to produce their edition with a 'best' text and notes of variations. This was issued in 12 volumes, including the index, between 1810 and 1828. There are some discrepancies in the numbering of acts of parliament between *Statutes of the realm* and *Statutes at large* because there are, in fact, two sources for what may be termed the original acts of parliament from the late fifteenth century. From 1497 the original bill with interlineated amendments and certified with the royal assent has been preserved in what is now the House of Lords Record Office (HLRO) and these are known as the Original Acts. From even earlier (1483) at the end of each session a transcript of the whole acts of the session was engrossed, signed and certified by the Clerk to the Parliaments and delivered into Chancery and kept in the Rolls Chapel and later at The National Archives (TNA). Inevitably there are minor discrepancies in the texts between the two sets but more importantly their arrangements are not identical and the consequential numbering of acts sometimes varies. The instances of this are not numerous compared to the whole but are sufficient to cause difficulties. Since 1849 both manuscript sets have been superseded by authenticated printed copies on vellum deposited in the HLRO and TNA.

As early as 1557 an attempt was made to produce an edition of the statutes which included only those acts which were still in force (William Rastell's *A Colleccion of all the statutes (from the begynning of Magna Carta unto the yere of our Lorde 1557 which were before that yere imprinted*). By the second half of the nineteenth century there was a desperate need for an authoritative version of something similar. In 1870 was begun *The Statutes revised* which omitted all acts that had been wholly repealed (and also all local, personal and private acts) and included those in force as they had been amended to date. The 18 volumes took 15 years to complete and by the end the earlier volumes were seriously out of date. A new edition was shortly produced, revised to 1886 and published in 16 volumes between 1888 and 1901 with supplements down to 1920. A third (and final) edition was published in 32 volumes in 1951, revised to 31st December 1948.

The deficiencies of these editions of *The Statutes revised* in terms of currency had long been recognised and in 1972 a replacement was started. Called *Statutes in force*, it was a loose-leaf edition to be continuously updated. Each act was issued in pamphlet form incorporating amendments to date with punched holes for filing in subject-arranged binders. After substantial amendment, an act would be reprinted as amended and would be inserted in the relevant binder replacing the unamended version of the act. Minor amendments were accommodated by filing update sheets at the front of the relevant binder. The system worked tolerably well until the early 1990s when amendments ceased on anticipation of the production of an electronic version (and because staff doing the updating were diverted to working on its electronic replacement). New acts were still issued in the *Statutes in force* format until 1996 but amended acts were not replaced and this is now as obsolescent as the former *The Statutes revised*. Meanwhile the electronic edition of the statutes in force has yet to be issued. It was promised originally for the mid 1990s and thereafter promised each year 'by the end of the year'; it has still not been published. In the meantime commercial editions of the statutes in electronic form proliferate (see Chapter 8).

So far we have only considered 'public general' acts – those acts of parliament concerned with stating or changing the laws of the land which affect all or most of us and are enacted by bills introduced within the Houses of Parliament. There are two other categories – private acts, and local and personal acts which grew out of them. A private act does not alter the law of the land but grants to the petitioner a privilege or exemption with respect to it. The bill is introduced from outside Parliament by petition praying that it may be given effect by Parliament. What this entails can best be explained by example. A railway company could in theory build a railway without recourse to legislation; in practice, it could hardly purchase the land *en route* without being held to ransom. A private act of parliament can grant the company power, among other things, of compulsory purchase upon conditions that, hopefully, can be equitable to all. While the particular act gives a defined and particular power of compulsory purchase it has not altered the law in general which prevents any private citizen or any group of them taking the land of another against his will.

Private acts were first recognised as a distinct class of acts in 1539 and thereafter they were numbered and listed in the sessional volumes of (public) acts but, as explained above, not published there or anywhere else. From the late seventeenth century, there were an increasing number of private acts for which non-publication was a real problem. They affected a wider range of the general public and litigation was more likely (in courts, private legislation was treated as 'evidence' and a copy of the relevant act certified by the Clerk to the Parliaments to be a 'true copy' had to be produced). To secure publication a fiction was introduced in the form of an additional clause in the bill that the act was to be deemed and taken as a public act. Most such acts, though by no means all, were acts establishing turnpike trusts to build or improve and maintain roads, or acts renewing their powers (which normally ran only for 14 years) and these 'private acts declared public' were generally known as 'Road Acts'.

Once the usefulness of this fiction was appreciated, the number of such acts grew apace to the displeasure of the Treasury who distributed a considerable quantity of public acts to MPs and to courts. The Treasury at first tried to leave such acts unpublished but that defeated the whole purpose of declaring them public and the attempt was abandoned. In 1753 a compromise was reached whereby two volumes of public acts were produced, the first for 'genuine' public acts and widely distributed and the second for acts quaintly described as 'public acts not printed in the general collection' with a much smaller print run and distribution list. Both categories continued to be numbered in a single sequence but the 'Road Acts' were gathered together at the end of the sequence so that the chapter number of public acts no longer reflected the chronology of their passing. In 1797, the two volumes of public acts were reorganised as two separate series of acts, each with their own numbering. Acts in the main volume were henceforward 'Public *general* acts' and those 'not printed in the general collection' (or Road Acts) became '[Public] local and personal acts'.

Ironically, within twenty years (in 1815, to be precise) private acts too began to be published, although not all that were passed were published until 1922. Initially they were numerous but gradually their numbers dwindled as non-legislative means were found to secure the same objectives. After 1844 foreigners did not need a naturalisation act to become British subjects as a Home Office certificate sufficed. A few years later (1857) divorce acts became a thing of the past when the same could be achieved by a judicial process. In other cases, the objective itself became obsolete. As more and more land was enclosed, less and less remained to be enclosed and fewer and fewer Inclosure acts (always spelt with an 'I') were passed. By the twentieth century private acts (from 1948 re-named personal acts) were rare and none has been passed for over 15 years.

In addition to the official texts of the statutes, there are a number of commercially produced unofficial editions issued with the authorisation of the King's/Queen's Printer. The texts are equally reliable and can be used by anyone with confidence that they are authentic. Indeed, they are routinely used by the legal profession in preference to the official editions. They generally have two advantages lacking in official editions – they incorporate amendments and they are annotated. Long before the production of *Statutes in force* and before even the production of *The statutes revised*, lawyers felt the need for editions which omitted repealed acts and included others as they were currently in force and which were subject arranged rather than in chronological order. Moreover, while courts cannot overturn acts of parliament, they can and must interpret what is seldom self-evident. According to the settled principles of English Common Law, such interpretations become part of the law of the land and bind courts in determining future cases and so another feature of such editions is their interpretative annotations.

Strictly, *Statutes at large* in its various editions is an unofficial text and a 'lawyers' edition', but it neither revised nor annotated the original texts of acts and remained chronologically arranged. It has, in any case, gained a semi-official status, being the preferred text in courts of law for acts passed between the end of 1713 (*Statutes of the realm*) and the first Parliament of the United Kingdom in 1801 (*Public general acts*).

The best-known 'lawyers' edition' of the statutes is *Halsbury's statutes* or, more fully, *Halsbury's Statutes of England and Wales*, a qualification that is important. It excludes all acts concerned exclusively with Scotland and Northern Ireland. It also excludes local, personal and private acts and 'certain minor acts' or acts 'of limited interest' including public acts of a local character. New editions of *Halsbury's statutes* are produced at long intervals but, in between, individual volumes are reissued thoroughly revised as necessary and annual supplements and 'noter-up' volumes cope with lesser or more recent amendments. The current edition is the 4th edition which began in 1985. The first important 'lawyers' edition' of the statutes was *Chitty's Statutes of practical utility* begun in the mid-nineteenth century. As the name suggests, it was a selective edition of acts of parliament and was subject arranged which was an innovation. It reached a 6th edition begun in 1911 but then ceased. Halsbury (1st ed., 1929–47) was effectively its successor. Another unofficial edition is *Current Law Statutes annotated* (1975–94) covering acts from 1973 to 1993 continued as *Current Law Statutes* (1995–). Although the long promised official version of *Statutes in force* online has not yet appeared, there are unofficial online editions available (see Chapter 8).

Statutes or acts of parliament are the most important enacted laws of the country and, for that reason, they are called 'primary' legislation. They are accepted as law by the courts and cannot be challenged and cannot be altered save by the authority of another act of parliament. (Since Britain's accession to the European Communities, now European Union, in 1973, that statement needs qualifying – within the scope of their competence, EU laws prevail over British legislation in cases of discrepancy). But there is a large body of enacted legislation besides acts of parliament and this is generically known as secondary or subordinate legislation. Most of it is delegated legislation; that is, it is specifically authorised by a 'parent' act of parliament. Detailed as many acts of parliament are, they can seldom be detailed enough and it is the practice for acts to permit authorities to 'fill in the details'. The act will specify which authority can make the necessary subordinate legislation (usually a minister of the crown (in effect, a government department) or the crown itself (Her Majesty in Council)) and the scope of the legislation authorised. Not all subordinate legislation is delegated; some authorities besides Parliament have inherent law-making powers of their own – local and public authorities have the power to make by-laws, courts can make their own binding rules and the Crown retains a residue of its power (the 'royal prerogative') to make laws from the days when it, and not parliament, was the principal law-making authority for the country. However, nowadays, all by-laws and court rules are made under statutory authority as are many instruments of the royal prerogative and these are no different in status to any other delegated legislation. There remain some prerogative instruments that are not delegated.

The majority of instruments of delegated legislation are issued as 'Statutory instruments' (SIs), known before 1948 as 'Statutory Rules and Orders' (SR&Os). These began as a numbered series (the numbers begin at the start of each calendar year) in 1894. They existed, of course, before then but without any system; they were unnumbered, published in a variety of ways or, all too often, not published at all. Like acts of parliament, there are public and local SR&Os or SIs but they number in a single annual sequence. SIs are first issued as separate instruments ranging from a single sheet to a publication of several hundred pages but some local SIs, indeed most of them, remain unpublished. Subsequently they are reissued in an annual volume (nowadays several volumes per year). Those local SIs that were separately published are omitted from the annual volumes as are what are called temporary instruments (those revoked or spent within the year). The annual volumes of SR&Os, later SIs, actually begin before the start of a numbered series as the Treasury issued annual volumes of subordinate legislation with the title *Statutory rules and orders* from 1890 to 1893. Earlier instruments still in force were gathered together in 8 volumes and issued in 1896 as *Statutory rules and orders other than those of a local, personal and temporary character issued prior to 1890 and now in force.* Any instruments that had been amended were printed in their amended and not in their original form. Another edition, revised to 1903, was published in 13 volumes in 1904 and a third edition, revised to 1948, was published in 25 volumes in 1949–52. No further edition has been published but Butterworths has published *Halsbury's Statutory instruments* (with similar exclusions to *Halsbury's Statutes*). The current edition (called the 'grey volumes' as opposed to the 'black volumes' of the previous edition) was issued from 1986 in 22 volumes plus updates.

Not all delegated legislation is issued in the form of statutory instruments and not all subordinate legislation is delegated but, although there are surprisingly numerous categories of subordinate legislation that do not qualify as SIs, they seldom concern the general public. Some apply only to a restricted group of citizens (e.g. *The Queen's regulations for the Army* and equivalent regulation for the Navy and for the Air Force, or the Orders of Council which regulate the medical and dental professions) or are geographically restricted like local authority by-laws or compulsory purchase orders, or departmental orders (called 'sealed orders' because they bear the seal of the authorising department) affecting boundary revisions. Yet others, though issued by a 'British' authority, the Crown, apply to colonial possessions, such as letters patent or orders-in-Council establishing colonial constitutions. Others again shade from legislation into administrative action – is a royal proclamation dissolving Parliament and calling fresh elections really legislation? These and other categories of ephemeral non-SI subordinate legislation are discussed succinctly in a useful handout issued by the British Library's Social Sciences and Official Publications department – *Legislation of the United Kingdom* (How to find official publications in the Official Publications and Social Sciences Reading Area; 3).

Finding what you want among the legislation of this country is never easy and, if the result affects you personally (if you need to know how you stand with respect to the law), you would do well to seek legal advice. The law involves not just legislation but case law as well and, even if you track down the relevant texts, they need to be interpreted. Initially the advice from a Citizen's Advice Bureau or a law centre may suffice but, if litigation is in prospect, the advice of a solicitor is probably necessary. Nevertheless, there are plenty of occasions when you may want to track down particular pieces of legislation for yourself.

There are several guides which are useful to clarify what you want or what exists and how it is organised. A good general guide to acts of parliament and more up-to-date than most is Gifford (D. J.) & Salter (J.) *How to understand an act of parliament*. London : Cavendish, 1996. A useful pamphlet is *Passing legislation in the United Kingdom*. London : Foreign & Commonwealth Office, 2000. An older work but still useful is Hughes (Christopher) *The British Statute book*. London : Hutchinson, 1957. More specialised is a pamphlet called *Acts of parliament : some distinctions in their nature and numbering* (House of Commons Library document; No.2, 1955) and several leaflets in the House of Commons Information Office (HCIO) 'Factsheets' series: *Parliamentary stages of a government bill* (L1), *Private members' bill procedure* (L2) (Private members' bills are *public* bills and not the same at all as Private bills), *Hybrid bills* (L5) and *Tracing acts of parliament* (L12). These and other HCIO Factsheets are available on the United Kingdom Parliament website at **http://www.parliament.uk/parliamentary_publications_and_archives/factsheets.cfm**. A good and brief guide to what exists is *Sweet & Maxwell's Guide to law reports and statutes*, 4th ed. London, 1962. Finally good starting points if you don't know where to begin are Walker (David M.) *The Oxford companion to the law*. Oxford : Clarendon Press, 1980 and Holborn (Guy) *Butterworth's legal research guide*, 2nd ed. London : Butterworths, 2001.

For private acts and local and personal acts there is *Private bill legislation (including Provisional orders and Special procedure orders)*. London : HMSO, 1953 issued by HM Treasury and the HCIO Factsheet *Private bills* (L4). For an historical study there is Lambert (Sheila) *Bills and acts : legislative procedure in the eighteenth century*. Cambridge : Cambridge University Press, 1971. For secondary or subordinate legislation there are *Subordinate legislation*. London : HMSO, 1951 (HM Treasury. Notes on government organisation…; No.10), *Access to subordinate legislation*. London : HMSO, 1963 (House of Commons Library document; No.5) and HCIO Factsheets: *Statutory instruments* (L7), *Church of England measures* (L10) and *Order confirmation…*(L9). Also of use is the section on subordinate legislation in *Halsbury's Laws of England* (4th ed. Reissue, Vol.44(1) (1995) 1499–1526 and *passim*) and the preliminary notes (pp.1–13 in vol.1) in Halsbury's *Statutory instruments…* grey volumes. General guides to British official publications, which will include sections on legislation, are mentioned in Chapter 4.

The main printed indexes to public general acts of parliament are twofold. First there is the *Index to the statutes* and then there is the *Chronological table of the statutes*. These began as a single publication in 1870 and new editions were issued at irregular intervals (now every two years) which split into two series in 1950. Both have their limitations as finding tools. The *Index* is a systematic index of acts as they are currently (at the cut-off date of that edition) in force. Each subject section is subdivided into more specific topics and if there is legislation concerning Scotland only or Northern Ireland, these follow the main sections for the subject. There are cross-references from subject terms not used to the used terms. The index is at the level of the section or sub-section or schedule of an act. Acts in the body of the index are identified by just their calendar year and chapter number but, at the head of each subject section, they are listed chronologically with their short titles. The *Index* contains no references to any acts no longer in force but the *Chronological table* includes all public acts. As the title suggests they are arranged chronologically, by regnal year to 1962 and calendar year thereafter, and then by chapter number. The table is much more than just a checklist of acts; it also indicates their status – those entirely repealed are set in *italic* type, those still in force, in whole or in part, are set in **bold** type. If nothing further is added to the latter, it indicates that the act remains in force exactly as passed but, if it has been amended or partially repealed, the sections affected are listed beneath the act concerned with the citation of the acts which made the changes. The *type* of change (amendment, repeal, *etc.*) is indicated but not the nature of the amendment.

If you do not know at least the approximate date of the act you are seeking, the *Chronological table* will not help and you will have to use the *Index* but, if the act you are seeking is no longer in force, it will not be there. If the library you are using still has them, you can use superseded editions of the *Index* for the period of your interest but, if this predates the earliest edition, you will have problems. A few earlier and less detailed indexes exist but in general you will have to use the acts themselves working backwards to see which later acts of relevance have amended or repeated earlier ones. In fact, nowadays, modern technology is a great help and online sources of acts (see Chapter 8) will be able to track back to earlier acts and will be able to provide an original or an 'as-amended' text.

The *Index* is concerned only with 'Statutes' which in this case means *public* acts and this is also so for the main sequence in the *Chronological table* but there is a sequence of local and personal acts at the back of the latter but this starts only from 1973. For long there was little for any earlier period but in the last few years this omission has been made good by two publications: *Chronological table of local legislation 1797–1994* (4 vols.). London : HMSO, 1996 and *Chronological table of private and personal acts 1539–1997*. London : TSO, 1999. In both cases, the start date is the date when that category of acts began. Supplements were published for the former but both titles are now available, updated to December 2002 at the time of writing, on the HMSO website at **http://www.legislation.hmso.gov. uk/legislation/chron-tables/chron-index.htm**

For nearly half a century the only index to local and personal legislation was *Index to local and personal acts 1800–1947*. This differs from the corresponding *Index to the statutes* in a number of important ways. It was a one-off and not an ongoing publication (though a supplement covering 1948–66 was eventually produced); for the period covered, *all* relevant acts and not just those in force were listed; the subject groups were very broad (all the thousands of railway acts were grouped together, for example) and acts within the groups were listed alphabetically; and it was the whole acts that were indexed without any attempt to analyse the contents. An exception to the last concerned Provisional orders, an early type of subordinate legislation that had to be confirmed by acts of parliament and were printed as a schedule to the confirming act. It was the orders not the acts that were indexed. Recently two almost identically named indexes have been published: *Index to local and personal acts 1850–1995* (4 vols.). London, HMSO, 1996 and *Index to local and personal acts 1797–1849* (2 vols.). London, TSO, 1999. Apart from the different period of coverage, these indexes are alphabetical and have not entirely superseded their predecessor. Two earlier indexes should be mentioned which predominantly include private acts: Bramwell (George) *Analytical table of private statutes 1727–1834* (2 vols.). London, 1893 and Vardon (Thomas) *Index to the local and personal and private acts 1798–1839*. London, 1840. A useful index of a specialised type of local act, the inclosure act, is Tate (W.E.) *A domesday of English enclosure* [sic!] *acts and awards*. Reading, University of Reading, 1978. This is particularly useful in giving locations for the awards which contain (as the acts do not) the maps which most enquirers are seeking.

The indexes to SIs, and to SR&Os before that, are similar to those for statutes. The *Index to government orders* also indexes only legislation in force. Although 'government orders' could be construed as covering all subordinate legislation, it does, in fact, only cover SIs and their predecessors. In one respect it differs from the *Index to the statutes*. While the latter does index public acts, the *Index to government orders* does not index the orders themselves but the authority for them. Orders under a subject heading are listed under the act which authorised them and, where an act has authorised subordinate legislation, it is listed even if, at the time of publication, no order has been made. The *Table of government orders*, like the corresponding table of statutes, is a chronological table but, unlike it, it is not a comprehensive list of every order ever issued. It includes all SR&Os and SIs in force on 31st December 1948 and all those published in the annual volumes from 1949 onwards; it, therefore, excludes all orders spent or revoked before 1949, all temporary orders and all local and private orders which explains the considerable gaps in the numbering in the table. Otherwise content and layout is similar to the statutes – italic for revoked orders and bold for those in force with effects listed underneath where relevant. Between 1952 and 1965 the 'table' and the 'effects' were in separate publications (*SI effects* and *Numerical table, SR&O and SI*), both annual. Since 1941, HMSO (now TSO) has issued a monthly list, now called *List of statutory instruments*, with annual cumulations. These include all SIs issued including local personal or private SIs, temporary SIs and even unprinted SIs (identified as such). All printed SIs (but not unprinted ones) are also included in HMSO/TSO's *Daily list* (see Chapter 4). A specialised index is Clinker (C. R.) *Light railway orders*. Bristol : Avon-Anglia Publications, 1977 and historical indexes of special types of subordinate legislation include: *Index to orders in council, proclamations* [etc.]... *published in the London gazette...*[1830–1883]. London : Council of Law Reporting, 1885, *Bibliography of royal proclamation of the Tudor and Stuart sovereigns* (Biblioteca Lindensiana; 5 & 6). 2 vols. and *Handlist of proclamations...* 1714–1910... (Biblioteca Lindensiana; 8).

A useful finding aid for British legislation of all sorts is the printed catalogue of the British Library: *General catalogue of printed books* where it is entered under the heading of ENGLAND. [LAWS AND STATUTES...] with various subdivisions for, among others, general collections, smaller collections, collections of laws on specific subjects and a chronological series; there is also a separate chronological listing of proclamations which runs to over 100 pages in the K. G. Saur reprint. Further listings of specialised laws can be found under the headings of ENGLAND. [DEPARTMENTS OF STATE, ETC. – ARMY. – REGULATIONS AND ORDERS...] divided into general regulations and regulations on special subjects. There are corresponding series for the Royal Navy and Royal Air Force and more laws under the headings for the service ministries (Admiralty, Air Ministry and War Office). The collection of legislation under a few headings systematically arranged means that the printed catalogues can be browsed in a way that the online catalogue cannot.

Chapter 2. Parliamentary proceedings

The documentation of what Parliament does constitutes the parliamentary proceedings which comprise principally two series for each House to which can be added the daily business papers of both. The first main series, the 'Journals', records what is done – decisions taken, motions and resolutions passed or rejected, the procedural stages of legislation, action on petitions and so on. Each House has its own – the *Journals of the House of Commons* and the *Journals of the House of Lords*. They are called 'Journals' as they are the day-to-day record of the activity of the House concerned while it sits; they are then published retrospectively at the end of each session. They are among the earliest of official publications dating from the sixteenth century (1509 (1510 New Style) for the House of Lords and 1547 for the House of Commons) although they existed only in manuscript until the mid-eighteenth century. Earlier journals were then printed for the first time and from then sessional volumes began to be printed and published shortly after the session they covered and this continues to this day.

Much later came the reporting of debates. This was illegal until the nineteenth century and, indeed, remains so without authorisation. Nevertheless, increasingly in the eighteenth century unofficial and clandestine reports were made and printed. These might report a single debate, the debates of a period, usually a fairly brief period, or on a particular topic. But even in aggregate, they did not constitute a continuous or systematic report of parliamentary debate. Nevertheless most of what did exist was gathered at the turn of the century by William Cobbett and reprinted as Cobbett's *Parliamentary history*. In 1803, following upon his *Parliamentary history*, Cobbett began publishing his *Parliamentary debates*. At first, like the *History*, his *Debates* reprinted the reports of others, this time the contemporary reports in newspapers. After eight years Cobbett was bought out by T. C. Hansard in 1811. Cobbett's volumes were reprinted and continued as *Hansard's Parliamentary debates*. A 'New Series' was begun with the opening of the reign of George IV (1820) and a 'Third Series' with that of William IV (1830) but this continued down to 1892 when Parliament, dissatisfied with the reporting of its debates, put the contract out to tender and Hansard lost. The 'Fourth Series', the first to be called 'Authorised', nevertheless was very similar to the previous series.

All four series share certain characteristics. Firstly the debates of both Houses were reported in the same volume. For any day on which both Houses sat, the debates of the House of Lords, the upper house, were reported first followed by those of the House of Commons; then followed the debates of each House for the next day and so on. The debates were not verbatim; those of the principal speakers were substantially so but backbenchers' speeches were summarised and reported in the third person. Finally in 1908, these two defects – one an inconvenience, the other a serious defect – were reviewed again by Parliament which decided to take over its own reporting. From 1909, two series were produced, one for each House and the reporting of the debates were for the first time designated 'Official report'. Most of all, however, the debates were reported verbatim, or substantially so. Most repetitions and omissions and the 'ums' and 'ahs' of ordinary speech are silently corrected but nothing of substance is added or omitted. Despite the fact that Hansard's connexion with reporting the debates ceased in 1892, the printed reports continued to be known colloquially as 'Hansard' and in 1943 the name was restored to the title-page.

Nowadays *Hansard* is first produced in a daily edition which is printed overnight and is available in the morning for the previous day's debates. For debates during a late-night or all-night sitting, there is a 10 p.m. cut-off for the *Hansard* published the next morning and debates after that are issued with the debates of the next day. 'Weekly Hansard' consists of unrevised daily reports for the week bound together with a paper cover. The permanent record is the bound volumes usually covering two weeks' debates (three weeks for the House of Lords) and incorporating corrections of errors found in the unrevised daily/weekly *Hansard*. In addition to recording actual speeches *Hansard* has for long included written answers to questions in both the daily/weekly and the permanent bound volumes. These comprise both answers which were requested in written form and those for which an oral reply was sought but which was not reached in the limited period available daily for questioning ministers.

Besides the *Parliamentary debates* of each House, there is a third series of debates, much less well known than the other two but, because of a 1992 judicial decision of the House of Lords (*Pepper v. Hart*) which permitted debates on a bill to be used to interpret acts, these are becoming more important. This is the *Standing Committee debates* (SCD) of the House of Commons. Traditionally the committee stage of a bill was taken on the floor of the House. The House resolved itself into a 'Committee of the Whole House', the Speaker stepped down and was replaced by his deputy and the rules of debate were somewhat relaxed. This remains so for the House of Lords and exceptionally for the Commons as well. Bills of constitutional significance and the annual Finance Bill (nowadays only parts of it) have their Committee stage on the floor of the House. By contrast, wholly uncontroversial bills (often private members' bills) and occasional emergency bills, where little or no debate is anticipated at Committee stage, are also taken on the floor of the House. Otherwise because of pressure of business (exacerbated in the late nineteenth century by filibustering tactics of Irish Nationalist MPs) the committee stages of most public bills are remitted to actual committees.

Originally a committee for this purpose was established at the start of a parliamentary session and considered whatever bills were remitted to it until the session ended (hence 'standing' committee). Soon several were needed and they were identified by letters, Standing Committee 'A', 'B', 'C', … These committees are relatively large (20–40 members), are non-specialist, and reflect *pro rata* the political composition of the House as a whole. Nowadays committees are constituted *ad hoc* for each bill and though lettered designations have been retained, there is no continuity and the term 'Standing Committee', though still the official designation, is now a misnomer. The printing of debates of each standing committee began in 1919 and they are issued daily for the previous day's sittings as with the main *Hansard* but there is no 'weekly SCD' and the bound volumes cover the debates of the whole session and are published literally years in arrears.

Since the start of the 1999–2000 session another series of debates has existed. Again, pressure of business is the cause. Certain business of the House of Commons is now taken in the Grand Committee Room in Westminster Hall in parallel with the main debates in the House of Commons proper. A decision was taken at the time that these debates would not be recorded in yet another separate series but would be included in the main debates of the House of Commons though in a separately numbered sequence with the column numbers identified with the prefix 'WH' for 'Westminster Hall'.

The business papers of the House of Commons constitute a complicated, rare and little known series of printed documents collectively known as 'The Vote' or 'The Vote bundle'. The series started in the 1680s as *The Votes*, later *Votes and proceedings*, which were the daily minutes of the previous day's sitting. It therefore does on a daily basis what the *Journals* do for the session. Nowadays both use the same format for compilation, though this was not always the case, and therefore the latter is now a straightforward cumulation of the former. If this were all, the votes would be of only passing interest, useful until the publication of the *Journals* but there is more to the Vote bundle. From the late eighteenth century various 'Appendices' and 'Supplements' were included with *The Votes* and from 1817 various agenda papers were included as well. These now include the Order Paper (that day's agenda), Private Business, the Notice Paper (giving notice of motions and questions), Standing Committee Proceedings, Public Bill List, European Communities Documents List and Supplements to the Votes (containing proposed amendments to bills). Since 1997 the arrangement has been somewhat simplified.

Formerly other series were included. From 1833 to 1974 the *Report of the Select Committee on Petitions* was included. For much of the nineteenth century the number of petitions was vast but they subsequently dwindled and the Select Committee was wound up in 1974. Nowadays petitions are printed as supplements to *Votes and proceedings*. It should be noted that the names of petitioners have never been printed and even the actual text of petitions has not always been given in full. From 1836 to 1994 Division Lists were included in the Vote bundle and from 1892 to 1915 written answers to parliamentary questions. Both were also printed in *Hansard* and eventually their separate publication was discontinued.

The House of Lords' equivalent to the Commons' Vote bundle is their *Minutes of proceedings* which has been printed only from 1824, and between 1838 and 1929 was reprinted as a parliamentary paper in the House of Lords' sessional papers (see Chapter 3). Unlike the Vote bundle, *Minutes of proceedings* has little supplementary material and only one sub-series has regularly been issued – *List of rules, orders, etc.* (after 1948 *Statutory instruments, etc.*) has appeared since 1907.

How to find the various series of parliamentary proceedings is not difficult. All are major series and the catalogues of any holding libraries will include details. The *Parliamentary debates* (Hansard) are very widely available, especially for recent years. Libraries holding the *Journals* of the House of Lords and the House of Commons are fewer but the majority of academic libraries and the major public libraries should have copies. It is far otherwise with the Vote bundle. In London, apart from in the Houses of Parliament, the British Library alone currently has a set and in the country as a whole there are probably only half a dozen current sets, mostly in the Copyright Libraries.

'How to find', however, in the context of parliamentary proceedings, means how to find information within the relevant series and how to find what is the relevant series for the information sought. Leaving aside the business papers (the Vote bundle) for the moment, the distinction that has to be made is that the *Journals* record is what is *done* in the House and the Debates what is *said*. There are, it is true, some small exceptions to this. The Queen's speech, for example, setting out the government's programme for the session is 'said' in the House of Lords and should be found in the debates of that House. So it is, but it is also to be found in the Commons' *Debates* and in the *Journals* of both Houses. Likewise a Division, a vote upon a motion, is an action – something 'done' and, as such, will correctly be found in the *Journals* of the relevant House. But all that will be found there is the text of the motion and the result – the number of votes cast for and against and whether the motion was lost or won – no names, except for the tellers (who do not vote), are given. For the *names* of those who voted 'aye' or 'no', you will have to consult *Hansard*.

Once you have decided whether it is the *Journals* or *Hansard* that you want, each series has its own integral indexes. Each sessional volume of the *Journals* of each House has its own index and these are in time cumulated into separately issued 10-year indexes which go back to the late nineteenth century. Before that the cumulative indexes cover longer and more irregular periods. The indexes, indeed the *Journals* themselves, are not easy to use as they have changed little in centuries and now appear archaic. The indexes are part alphabetic subject and part systematic with headings for categories like 'petitions' or 'bills' but, once you have mastered them, they are often sufficiently detailed that there is no need to refer to the actual entries in the *Journals* themselves. If, for example, you wish to follow the progress of a bill through the House, the index not only gives you the column reference but the date for each stage of a bill – the three readings, the committee and report stages, the consideration of the other House's amendments and the royal assent. To see the full progress of a bill, you will have to consult the indexes to the *Journals* of both Houses.

The daily issues of *Hansard* are unindexed and *Weekly Hansard* is simply five daily issues stapled together but fortnightly indexes are separately published to the daily parts fairly promptly. The fortnight covered by these indexes are the same two weeks that later comprise the period covered by the permanent bound volumes of the House of Commons' *Hansard* and the index to the bound volume supersedes the separate fortnightly indexes in the same way as the bound volumes supersede the daily/weekly issues. At the end of a parliamentary session, a cumulative index is produced covering all the volumes of that session and this is normally issued as a separate index volume. With one exception there have never been any indexes cumulating longer periods than a session. The exception goes back to the start of the series and there is an index covering the first and new [second] series, 1803–30 but this was not repeated for later periods. In the early 1990s, Chadwyck-Healey Ltd advertised their intention to produce a CD-ROM index to *Hansard* down to 1940 but nothing came of this.

The indexes are both a subject index to the topics of debates, statements, questions, etc. and a name index of speakers in a single alphabetical sequence. The subject element of the index is not analytical – it is the subject of the debate (etc.) as a whole that is indexed and not the various discrete matters raised in the course of the debate. The title of the debate as down on the order paper will give the heading for the debate in *Hansard* and will provide the index term. In the case of debates on bills, the title of the bill will provide the term in the index. The Commons' *Hansard* has two sequences and more recently three. In the main sequence (the debates proper) the columns (NB not pages) are numbered in standard Arabic numerals and this is followed by a sequence for written answers with column numbers in italic Arabic numerals. The indexes used to follow the same system. The italic numeration for written answers were identifiable enough if you were aware of the systems and looking out for the distinction but it was far from obvious otherwise and gave rise to considerable problems for the unwary. As a consequence from the start of 1983 the index entries for written answers abandoned giving column references with italic numerals and instead gave them in standard Arabic form with a small 'w' following – 123w, not *123*. The actual column numbers for written answers remain italic. Since December 1999 a third sequence, inserted between the other two contains the Westminster Hall debates and the column numbers are in standard Arabic numbers with capital 'WH' following and the index follows the same practice.

The indexes to the House of Lords' *Hansard* are essentially the same except that the bound volumes normally cover three weeks' debates instead of two; written answers, though still at the back of each volume, are not in a separate sequence; and there is no equivalent of Westminster Hall debates. There is but one sequence of column numbering and there is no need in the index to distinguish, as in the Commons' *Hansard*, 123, *123*, 123w and 123WH. *Standing Committee debates* are unindexed. These consist of debates on motions to amend bills and, in terms of subject access, the table of contents listing bills considered by the Committee concerned gives as much information as a *Hansard* index which does not analyse contents below the level of a bill. It is, however, still necessary to discover which Committee dealt with which bill. The *Journals of the House of Commons* will record that information and the index to it will be sufficient for the purpose but since 1983–84 there is a source that is much easier to use. The *Weekly information bulletin* (see Chapter 3) in each issue lists all the bills introduced in either House with details of their progress to date. For completed sessions, the same information is given as of the end of the session in the *Sessional information digest*. The date at which each stage of a bill is taken is given and, for the Committee Stage in the House of Commons, which Standing Committee considered the bill (or whether it was considered in the whole House) is also given.

For pre-Hansard (or pre-Cobbett) parliamentary debates, Cobbett's *Parliamentary history* should generally be sufficient for most people's needs, but sometimes it is desirable to go back to the original reports of debates that Cobbett used for his *History*. Moreover, there exist some reports unknown to Cobbett and in some instances there were two or more separate reports of the same debate with differences. The House of Commons Library has produced two useful bibliographies in its *House of Commons Library Document* series: *A bibliography of Parliamentary debates of Great Britain* (1956), No.2 in the series, and *Debates and proceedings of the British Parliaments* (1986), No.16. In the same series (No.7) there is *The Journal of the House of Commons: a bibliographical and historical guide* (1971).

There are no indexes to the Vote bundle. There were attempts in the distant past to produce indexes but little came of them and what little exists is extremely rare and can be safely ignored. Though the Vote bundle is useful to MPs on the day of issue, it is of limited use to anyone thereafter and most of the information of continuing usefulness will be reissued in more accessible form. The daily *Votes and proceedings* is superseded by the Sessional *Journals of the House of Commons*, the

Division lists and *Answers to written questions* (both now discontinued) also appear in *Hansard*, the daily *Minutes of Standing Committees* for each bill are superseded by more detailed minutes on the bill's whole committee stage issued as a parliamentary paper, and so on.

Two categories of information available from the Vote bundle and not elsewhere may be sought by enquirers – petitions and 'Early day motions' (EDMs). Petitions were once very numerous and there is a single cumulative index for the peak period for twenty years following the establishment of a select committee on petitions (1833–52). This was issued as a parliamentary paper (P.P.1854–55 (531) liv.1 – see Chapter 3). No further cumulations were produced and, although the numbers of petitions were beginning to drop, this is a real problem for the rest of the century and the indexes to the individual sessional reports of the Committee on Petitions are all that is available. By the twentieth century petitions had become few enough for browsing to be feasible.

Early day motions are motions put down for debate 'at an early day' (nowadays 'for which no day has been fixed') and in either case this is a euphemism for 'never'. The purpose of EDMs is not actually to secure a debate but to test the support for particular propositions or to warn the government of the strength of feeling of backbenchers on particular subjects. There are no indexes as such to EDMs though lists are produced at irregular intervals. However EDMs are one category where electronic access is not just convenient or desirable but absolutely essential. The Early Day Motions Website at **http://edm.ais.co.uk/** gives access to EDMs back to the 1997/98 parliamentary session.

Chapter 3. Parliamentary papers – Information for Parliament

Compared to acts of parliament, parliamentary papers are relative late-comers and their first appearance proved a false dawn in two senses – their purpose was rather different to later parliamentary papers and their production was not sustained. The earliest papers issued by Parliament were produced at the beginning of the Civil War and were issued as part of the propaganda to foster support for the parliamentary cause. The output was considerable but at the Restoration, it ceased abruptly and virtually nothing recognisable as a parliamentary paper was thereafter produced for nearly half a century.

During the course of the eighteenth century, more and more papers were being produced for the information of Parliament and for parliamentarians, and increasingly being published and thus being made available to a wider public. Bills began to be printed (under standing orders from 1703, *private* bills had to be submitted to Parliament in printed form but, as these had to be printed by the petitioner (see Chapter 1) and not Parliament, they have never been recognised as 'parliamentary' or even official publications). The earliest parliamentary estimates, the Army Estimates, were printed in 1715. Reports of Select Committees began to be issued and the government began to present papers to parliament, notably treaties (see Chapter 5). At first the more important papers were ordered to be printed in the *Journals* (see Chapter 2) but separate publication also occurred and eventually became the norm. By the beginning of the nineteenth century the output of each parliamentary session had become considerable and the need to organise and systematise the publication of parliamentary papers had become pressing.

Firstly action was taken to preserve the papers produced up to then. A set of reports of Select Committees was reprinted in 15 large folio volumes, known as 'The First Series' covering the period 1715–1801 (further 'Series' followed but they duplicate the Bound Set (see below) and can be ignored). Also, from papers still in store, some half a dozen sets of eighteenth-century papers were put together in 111 volumes under the auspices of Speaker Abbott and these are known as 'The Abbott Collection'. The sets comprise papers of all sorts and not just select committee reports and cover the period 1731–1800. No two sets are identical and no set is absolutely complete. The First Series is now rare and the Abbott Collection rarer still, and eighteenth-century papers survive that are not found in either, so that a modern facsimile reprint in 145 volumes, plus two volumes of indexes containing all known separately published papers of the House of Commons, is invaluable. Called *House of Commons sessional papers of the eighteenth century.* Wilmington, Del. : Scholarly Resources, 1975–76, it was edited by Sheila Lambert and is popularly known as the 'Lambert Reprint'. It does not include papers printed originally in the *Journals of the House of Commons* but references to these *are* included in the index which includes another most useful feature – it includes references to all 'papers' for which an order to print has been found in the *Journals* but for which no extant copy can be traced. These may never have been printed, despite the orders, or all copies may have been lost; either way it is worth knowing that, after an exhaustive search by the leading authority for the period, no copy has been found.

From 1801, at the end of each parliamentary session, the parliamentary papers of that session have been gathered together, sorted and bound in a prescribed order. The resulting volumes are known as the 'Bound Set'. That is the set in the House of Commons Library and other libraries with complete or near-complete sets will have bound them in the same order, aided by the issue of volume title-pages and tables of contents and, from 1807, sessional indexes, at first in manuscript. The arrangement of papers in the Sessional Volumes of the Bound Set until session 1978–79 was in four sequences – 'Public Bills', 'Reports of Committees' (i.e. of Select Committees of the House), 'Reports of Commissioners' (i.e. of any other enquiries) and 'Accounts and Papers' (i.e. all remaining papers). Within those four groups, the arrangement was alphabetical by subject and, where there were papers treating the subject exclusively with reference to Scotland or to Ireland or Northern Ireland, these followed papers treating the subject generally or with respect to England and Wales. This complicated arrangement was then abolished and from session 1979–80 papers have been arranged within sessions by paper series and then numerically. The British Library anticipated this arrangement by a few years (beginning it with session 1976–77) and most libraries with smaller collections have always arranged their collections by paper series and number.

Paper numbering began at the beginning of the nineteenth century, at the same time as the Bound Set and at first there was just two series – 'bills' (i.e. *public* bills; private bills were and are un-numbered and, as has been said, are not considered parliamentary papers) and 'papers' or House of Commons Papers. Numbering starts afresh with each parliamentary session. There is no fixed length for a session but Parliament is obliged to meet at least once a year and sessions tend to last about a year, nowadays from October or November to approximately the same time the following year. Formerly Parliament was not so busy and February to July was not unusual for a session. General elections may affect the pattern of sessions; if one is called in Spring or early Summer (as most are), it will bring the then session to a premature close and the first session of the new Parliament may be another short one, running to the following October/November or, more usually, an extra-long one running to the Autumn of the year following. Sessions are identified by the year or years in which they fall and, if two fall entirely within a single year, they are identified by that year plus 'session 1' or 'session 2'. Papers are therefore identified as, for example, Bill 21 of session 1975–76 (or '1975–76 Bill 21') or HC (House of Commons) Paper 123 of 1983–84 (or '1983–84 (123)').

In 1833, a third series was introduced called 'Command Papers'. These originate outside Parliament and are presented to it by the government (the formula printed on the paper is: 'Presented to the House of Commons by [name of minister by the office held] by command of Her Majesty', hence a 'command' paper. Command Papers had existed long before then but they had been numbered, when numbering started, as House of Commons papers. The new Command Papers had two characteristics: they numbered consecutively through successive sessions and their numbers were not printed on the Papers themselves. As a consequence, when cited, the paper number was put in square brackets. In 1870, this anomaly was rectified and command paper numbers were printed with a prefix 'C' (and the numbering started at 1 again). As the 'C' series started to approach 10,000 at the end of the century, a new 'Cd' series was begun at 1 again and as 10,000 was again approached in 1918, 1956 and 1987 further series started with different letter prefixes. So the following command papers: [1234], C 1234, Cd 1234, Cmd 1234, Cmnd 1234 and Cm 1234 all exist, all are different and are spread over a century and a half of publishing.

The volumes of the Bound Set are numbered; in fact, each is numbered twice. Each volume in each of the four groups ('bills', 'reports of committees', etc.) is numbered within its group but all the volumes of a session are also consecutively numbered. The volume number within a group is never used to identify the whereabouts of a paper, only the volume number within the session which, by convention, is numbered in lower case roman numerals, i.e. Vol.23 is cited as 'xxiii'. Each paper within the Bound Set also has two sets of page numbers – the original (printed) page numbers of the paper itself and the hand-written (later stamped) numbers of the pages within the made-up volume. It is the latter alone that should be used to identify the position of a paper within the Bound Set and it is the manuscript page number of the first page of a paper (usually the title-page) that is used for this purpose. The system sounds complicated but it pays to master it and it did allow for a succinct citation of a specific paper among the hundreds of thousands issued as parliamentary papers. Thus 'P.P. 1831–32 (141-V) xl 1' means that vol.5 of House of Commons' paper 141 of session 1831–32 is to be found at p.1 of vol.40 of the parliamentary papers of that session.

After 1978–79, the volume number of volume within the session and the page number within the volume become redundant as a means of locating a given paper within the Bound set and all that is now needed is the session and the paper series and number, e.g. 1991–92 HC37. Although Command Papers number independently of the parliamentary sessions and the session date is unnecessary for identification, it is still necessary under both systems to quote the session for retrieval purposes as they are still located among the papers of a specific session.

House of Lords' sessional papers are in principle little different from those of the House of Commons. There are far fewer of them. Bills are equally numerous in each House as bills have to pass through both Houses to become law but the Lords issue far fewer papers of their own. However, the main reason for the difference in size is that, although Command Papers are presented to both Houses of Parliament, they are not included in the Lords' set of sessional papers. Until 1988 bills and papers in the Lords' set were numbered in a single numerical sequence in each session and identified simply by the prefix HL; thereafter they numbered in two separate sequences identified as 'HL Bill' and 'HL Paper'. The parliamentary papers of the House of Lords are far rarer that those of the House of Commons and even where they can be found there may be further complications. The set in the British Library, for example, is not as complete as that for the House of Lords and, for historical reasons, was bound in a different sequence to the official set in the House of Lords, necessitating an extra 'look-up' stage to finding the British Library's copy. It is useful to know that in the nineteenth century it was commonplace for each House to communicate its papers to the other. Thus House of Lords paper 329 of 1867, a 'return' (a reply to a request or demand for information) on enclosures in the New Forest in vol.xix of the House of Lords Bound Set is also to be found as a House of Commons paper in vol.lix of 1867 of the Commons' Bound Set and for most people it will be this copy of the paper that will be easiest to find.

On the whole, the parliamentary papers are well indexed and it is not too difficult to track down copies. Almost all the Civil War parliamentary papers that survive exist in a collection at the British Library called the 'Thomason Tracts' collected by George Thomason at the time. This includes a vast amount of pamphlet literature and is by no means confined to parliamentary papers. There is a two-volume index to the Thomason Tracts. The List and Index Society has produced two invaluable indexes of parliamentary papers covering the period from the Civil War to the mid-eighteenth century. The first is called *Printing for Parliament 1641–1700*. London : List and Index Society, 1988 (Special series; Vol. 20) which includes the relevant material from the Thomason Tracts, and the other is *List of House of Commons sessional papers 1701–1750*. London : Swift, 1968 (List and Index Society, Special series; Vol.1); both were compiled by Sheila Lambert. Indexes to the First Series and to the Abbott Collection exist as *General index to the reports of committees ... 1715–1801* and *Catalogue of papers printed by order of the House of Commons ... 1731–1800* respectively. In general it is preferable to use the two-volume index to the Lambert reprint which were issued as un-numbered volumes of that edition. These are detailed if complicated and the volumes include a good guide to the edition.

From 1807, the Bound Set included indexes to each session which soon constituted the final volume of the session. In 1826 a cumulative index which covered all the Bound Set back to 1801 was issued and at irregular intervals ever longer cumulations were produced culminating in a three-volume index to 1852 which superseded all others; the *General index to bills … 1801–1852*, the *General index to the reports of Select Committees … 1801–1852* and the *General index to accounts and Papers [etc.] … 1801–1852*. The next cumulation covered 1852–69 and thereafter successive cumulations covered a decade.

The first four of these cumulations (for 1852–69 and the decennial cumulations for the 1870s to the 1890s) were, in turn, superseded by another (nearly) half-century cumulation: *General alphabetical index … 1852–1899*. Likewise the five decennial indexes for the first half of the twentieth century were replaced by the *General alphabetical index … 1900–1949*. There are decennial indexes for the 1950s, '60s and '70s but thereafter only uncumulated sessional indexes. The layout and arrangement of these official indexes has changed little over some 200 years. The indexes are alphabetical subject indexes with limited cross-references from unused terms. The terms themselves tend to be old fashioned or just plain idiosyncratic (India, for example, up to independence in 1947 was indexed under 'East India' as papers were originally concerned with the affairs of the *East* India Company). The arrangement under a given term is by the four groups by which the papers are organised – bills, reports of committees, reports of commissioners and accounts and papers – and Scotland and Ireland form separate subdivisions. Within these the arrangement is chronological. The indexes are now available online (see Chapter 8) and if you are searching for a specific paper this is the best way to find it but printed indexes still retain some advantages when searching for papers on a given topic.

There are some useful non-official indexes. Chadwyck-Healey, which has issued a complete set of Parliamentary Papers in microfiche, 1801 to date, has also published an index covering the whole of the nineteenth century: *Subject catalogue of the House of Commons Parliamentary Papers, 1801–1900* edited by Peter Cockton. Cambridge, 1988. The same publisher also issues *Index to the House of Commons Parliamentary Papers on CD-ROM, 1801–1999*. There is another index associated with a reprint edition. In the 1960s the Irish Universities Press published a selective edition of nineteenth-century papers and in connexion with this published both a *Catalogue of British Parliamentary papers in the IUP 1000 volume series* and a *Check List …* The first is an alphabetical subject index, the other a chronological list. There are several more specialised indexes both official and non-official. These include the *Index to the report by the Charity Commissioners*

[1819–43], the *Index to reports of Commissioners 1812–1840* (on the colonies), the *Index to Consular* [or trade] *reports 1869–1916* and a *Finding list of British Royal Commissions reports 1860–1935* among the official indexes, and among the non-official indexes are Adam (M.I.) et al. *Guide to the principal Parliamentary papers relating to the Dominions 1812–1911*. Edinburgh : Oliver & Boyd, 1913, Rodgers (Frank) *Serial publications in the British Parliamentary papers 1900–1968*. London : Library Association, 1971, Di Roma (E.) & Rosenthal (J.A.) *Numerical finding list of British Command papers 1833–1961/62*. New York, 1967 continued by McBride (Elizabeth A.) *British command papers ... 1962/63–1976/77*. Atlanta, [1982] and the Library Association's *British government publications : an index of chairmen, (1801–1982)* in 4 volumes, 1974–84, which covers but is not confined to parliamentary papers.

The House of Lords' Bound Set of its parliamentary papers has its own repertoire of indexes, at least for the earlier period. There are three cumulative indexes – *General index to the sessional papers ... House of Lords ... 1801–1859, 1859–1870* and *1871–1885*. After this there are only the indexes or tables of contents to individual sessions or more general indexes such as the HMSO catalogues (see Chapter 4). Otherwise one is reduced to browsing the Lords' Bound Set, provided one has access to it.

A most important guide and index, wider in scope than just parliamentary papers, is the *Weekly information bulletin (WIB)* issued weekly (as the name implies) since November 1978 while the House of Commons is sitting by the House of Commons Information Office. Issued on Saturdays, it contains details of the previous week's business of the House of Commons and the forthcoming business of both Houses for the following week. It regularly updates information on the progress of public and private bills going through Parliament, gives information on delegated legislation, lists standing and select committees with their business and membership and Lord's committees, gives bibliographical information on recent White Papers, Green Papers, EU documentation and Early Day Motions (EDMs), and miscellaneous information about MPs, by-elections, the House of Commons and access details (postal addresses and Internet access). Issues from October 1996 onward are available on the UK Parliament website at **http://www.parliament.the-stationery-office.co.uk/pa/cm/cmwib.htm**. The *WIB* is supplemented by the annual *Sessional information digest (SID)*. This is not strictly a culmination of the *WIB*. Some of the information is cumulated (data on legislation, for example) but in other cases the *Digest* provides a kind of index to the *Bulletin* (for White Papers and Green Papers, for example) and in some instances provides entirely new data such as a statistical analysis of the sittings of the House and the statistics for parliamentary questions. Once again, issues are available on the UK parliament website from the 1995–96 session onwards at **http://www.publications.parliament.uk/pa/cm/cmsid.htm**.

Chapter 4.   Non-Parliamentary papers – Information provided by Government

Until the First World War most published government information, certainly all the more important documents, were parliamentary (see Chapter 3) – either they were supplied in answer to a request or order of parliament ('Returns') or were presented to Parliament by the relevant government departments ('Command Papers'). In 1922 however a decision was made at the instigation of the Treasury drastically to reduce the number of papers presented to Parliament. This was done as an economy measure as there was (and is) an extensive free circulation of parliamentary papers. From then, it was determined, Command Papers should consist only of documents required by Parliament as a basis for imminent action, normally in connexion with impending legislation. Other papers which might formerly have been parliamentary either ceased to be published at all (the fate of one or two long-running statistical series) or were in future issued by the government departments themselves. In the case of the published output of Royal Commissions, the reports themselves continued to be parliamentary as before, but the mass of supporting documentation, the 'evidence', which hitherto had been part of the especial strength of this sort of enquiry and had also been parliamentary, in future was to be published, if at all, by the relevant government department. In practice, the oral evidence, the transcripts of the interrogation of witnesses by the Commission, often called the 'Proceedings', has been less likely to be published, though sometimes it may be summarised in the body of the report. The written evidence, documents submitted to the Commission or commissioned by it, has generally been reprinted as non-parliamentary publications of the Commission itself, though sometimes a body submitting evidence undertakes its own publication either instead of or in addition to that of the Commission.

At about the same time this tendency for the scope of official publications to become more diffuse, less easy to control and in some instances to be actually reduced in output, was compounded by the unintended side-effect of another decision taken as an efficiency measure. The format of most government publications was reduced from folio to quarto. This applied especially to parliamentary publications which had been consistently of the larger format. Non-parliamentary publications had been more variable in size and there were instances, such as the Colonial Annual Reports, where the same documents were issued twice, once in folio as parliamentary papers (Command Papers) and once published in quarto by the Colonial Office in its own numbered series. Now non-parliamentary papers were standardised in the smaller format. This hastened the demise of some statistical series as this format was less suited to the tabular presentation of large-scale data. There were some exceptions, notably the Census Reports. These had hitherto been issued as parliamentary, the first censuses in England and Scotland, taken in 1801, coinciding nicely with the start of the present style of parliamentary publishing. They now became non-parliamentary but, because of the need to present large tables, they retained their folio format. All the censuses up to that of 1911, therefore, were parliamentary, including Irish censuses which began in 1821, and all from 1921 (there was none for Ireland that year and later ones covered only Northern Ireland) were non-parliamentary. In fact the rigid application of the new rules on the eligibility of Command Papers meant that one very late report of the 1911 census appeared as a non-parliamentary publication whereas the Preliminary Report of the 1921 census *was* parliamentary.

Although 1922 saw some diminution in official publishing (some statistical series and some Royal Commission evidence), this ran counter to the trend for an ever wider scope of government and of the issue of publications in support of this. Traditionally government had consisted of the defence of the realm externally, the maintenance of law and order internally and the raising of sufficient revenue to carry out these functions. Some expansion beyond this began early, such as trade protection and the administration of overseas possessions, but the big expansion began in the nineteenth century. The example of education as a subject of government was given in the introduction; other activities which became a matter of government concern were the working conditions in mines and factories, and sanitation and public health. The twentieth century has seen an expansion in government control or provision in areas such as pensions (disability and retirement), utilities and transport undertakings (some of these, like gas supply and tram services, were at least partly publicly run by the late nineteenth century but at the municipal rather than the national level), health (i.e. the provision of a health service, the NHS, and not just matters of public health), agriculture, consumer affairs, energy, industrial relations, planning, the environment, race relations, sport, the arts, and much more.

While the importance of parliamentary publications in the nineteenth century cannot be over-emphasised, there were some significant non-parliamentary publications issued. Examples of these are Admiralty pilots (e.g. *South American pilot. Pt I The east coast* … London, 1864, and *Pt II Sailing directions for South America, La Plata, etc.* London, 1848), Geological Survey publications (e.g. *Memoirs of the Geological Survey of Great Britain and of the Museum of Economic Geology.* London, 1846–), Board of Trade accident enquiries (e.g. *Reports on accidents to shipping, general series,* … *accidents to ships due to explosions,* and … *accidents to fishing vessels,* all 1888– (other accident enquiries, such as in mines, were usually parliamentary), and the *Board of Trade journal of tariff and trade notices.* London, 1886– (later simplified to the *Board of Trade journal* and still continuing after several changes of name consequent upon departmental changes). These examples might suggest that most non-parliamentary publications were scientific or technical in nature and many were, but not all; for example the Colonial Office's *Emigrants' Information Office handbooks*. London, 1888– and the rich collection of publications issued by the Record Commissioners and their successors, the Public Record Office. An early example of the latter is *Rymer's Foedera*, a collection of treaties published by the Record Commissioners in 4 vols., 1816–69. But this was not the first edition of this work; Thomas Rymer was commissioned by the crown in 1693 to compile it from the records then housed in the Tower of London and he published it in 17 volumes between 1704 and 1717; several more editions were produced in the eighteenth century including one published in The Hague.

Another rich source of early (and generally continuing) non-parliamentary publications are what may be called staff directories. The armed services were first in this field. The Annual Army List dated from 1754 (*A list of the general and field officers … [and] the officers in the several regiments of horse, dragoons and foot … on the British establishment …* London, 1754) and continued until 1868. It was joined in 1798 by the *Monthly army list* which continued (though latterly at lesser frequency) to 1958. In 1839 Hart's Quarterly Army List began and in 1840 Hart's Annual Army list, both called *The new army list*; they ceased in 1915. Finally the *Quarterly army list* began in 1880 and became the *Half-yearly army list* in 1922 until 1948. The following year it was replaced by the annual *The army list*. This was revised in 1951 and is issued in three parts (Pt I being the active list, annual to date, Pt II *Officers in receipt of retired pay*, annual 1968–73, thereafter every 3 or 4 years with supplements in between; Pt III *Gradation list* is not issued to the public). Thus for nearly half a century there has been only the one 'Army list' but before that there were two or more and for much of the nineteenth century four running concurrently. Navy lists are simpler. *Steel's original and correct list of the Royal Navy* (usually known just as 'Steel's Navy list'), 1783–1816 was replaced in 1814 by *The navy list*, quarterly to 1870 when it was split into two series, quarterly and monthly, 1870–1924, which recombined as a quarterly in 1924 until 1948 and has been annual since 1949. *The monthly air force list,* 1919–1930, became *The air force list* from 1931 but remained monthly until 1940 when there were six issues per year to 1944 and then four until 1949. Since 1949 it has been annual.

Various government departments produced their own directories, of which two only (now combined as one) need be noted. The *Foreign Office list* began in 1806 and continued to 1965; from 1966 it has been called the *Diplomatic service list*. This lists personnel of the Foreign Office (now Foreign and Commonwealth Office) and of British diplomats and consular staff abroad. Until 1950 it also listed foreign diplomats, etc. in London but these have, since 1951, been separately listed in the *London diplomatic list*, currently published half yearly. The *Colonial Office list* began in 1862 and continued until 1966. It merged with the *Commonwealth Relations Office Yearbook* (1966, continuing the *Commonwealth Relations Office list*, 1951–65) to form the *Commonwealth Office yearbook* (1967–68) but with a further merger this ceased publication and a directory of the colonial service was included in the *Diplomatic service list*. In the meantime the rest of the publication with encyclopaedia-style articles on Commonwealth countries and dependant territories has been issued in a publication currently called *The Commonwealth yearbook*, 1987– which continued a *Year book of the Commonwealth*, 1969–1986.

There were other departmental lists but these have ceased either because the department no longer existed (e.g. the India Office) or has left direct government service (the Post Office) or simply because there was no need for a departmental list when a general one existed for the whole of the government service – *The Civil Service year book*. This began life as the *British imperial calendar and Civil Service list* in 1809 and changed its name in 1974. It has traditionally been annual, occasionally with a second edition a year when changes have been extensive (usually after a change of government) but changes are now so frequent that it is currently issued twice a year. What all these series have in common is that they all began as private ventures; the *British imperial calendar*, for example, was only taken over by HMSO in 1935. However, it is reasonable to consider them 'official' from the start, not only because it is absurd to consider the same publication both official and non-official at different times, but because, even as private ventures, they could not be compiled without the official sanction of the relevant department which was also the source for the data contained in the publications.

The government is the principal source of statistics in an ever widening range of topics. The base sources for many of these are the censuses. There has never been a census for the United Kingdom as such. The first census was for Great Britain in 1801 despite the fact that Ireland had been united with it a few months before to form the United Kingdom. The census of Great Britain was continued decennially until 1851 and was joined by separate censuses of Ireland in 1821. In 1861 the Great Britain census was split into two – a census of England and Wales and a census of Scotland – and the three censuses (including Ireland) continued every ten years until 1911. In 1921 censuses were held in England and Wales and in Scotland but the disturbed situation in Ireland precluded a census there and the following year the Irish Free State separated from the UK leaving just Northern Ireland within it. Northern Ireland held a census in 1926 and again in 1937. The rest of the UK had censuses in 1931 but there was no census anywhere in the UK in 1941 because of the war. In 1951 for the first time since 1911 censuses were held in all the parts of the UK at the same time and this has continued every 10 years since then with a 10% sample census held in 1966 but not repeated. The early censuses were little more than headcounts but gradually more and more information was elicited and published. In recent decades the

Preliminary report has been followed by detailed statistics in county volumes where the breakdown is geographical and a range of topic volumes covering matters such as place of birth or travel to work. Since 1966 these have been supplemented by small area statistics (down to enumeration district or, in some instances, postcode levels) issued in a variety of non-print forms (microform and electronic). County volumes have not been published for the 2001 census and many of the results will only be available electronically (see Chapter 8).

There are a number of guides to the censuses. The main retrospective guide is *Guide to census reports, Great Britain, 1801–1966*. London : HMSO, 1977 which identifies all the census publications and describes changes in the scope of successive censuses; it supersedes a similar publication of 1951 covering the censuses to 1931. This can be supplemented by later guides on specific censuses such as the *Census users' handbook*, edited by Stan Openshaw. Cambridge : GeoInformation International, 1995 and *The 1991 census user's guide*, edited by Angela Dale and Catherine Marsh. London : HMSO, 1993.

After the census, the most important source of statistics is the *Annual abstract of statistics* which contains statistics on a wide range of topics usually covering a span of years to allow for comparisons (nowadays mostly for 11 years). This began in 1854 (covering 1840–53) as a parliamentary paper called *Statistical abstracts of the United Kingdom*. Unusually, it remained parliamentary after 1922 and continued until 1939 (covering 1924–38) when it was suspended for the war. It resumed after the war in 1947 as a non-parliamentary publication with its present title (No.84, 1935–46–). It has been supplemented since 1946 by the *Monthly digest of statistics*. Other general series of statistics are *Regional trends* issued annually by the Office for National Statistics (ONS) (until 2001, and then available only on the ONS website – see Chapter 8) and series like the *Digest of Welsh statistics* issued annually by the National Assembly for Wales, formerly the Welsh Office.

Statistics on narrower or more specialised matters abound and a few examples will suffice – *Abortion statistics* (ONS), annual; *Civil Judicial statistics, Scotland* (Scottish Executive), annual; *Community statistics* [for Northern Ireland] (Dept. for Health, Social Security and Public Safety, Belfast), annual; *Criminal statistics, England and Wales* (Home Office), annual; *Economic trends* (ONS), monthly with annual supplements; *Family spending* (ONS), annual; *Labour market trends* (ONS), monthly; *Monthly statistics of building materials and components* (DTI); *Family spending* (ONS), annual; *Population trends* (ONS), quarterly; *Work and pensions statistics* (DWP), annual; *Students in higher education institutions* (Higher Education Statistics Agency), annual; *Overseas trade statistics* (Customs and Excise) in various series, monthly, quarterly and annual; and the *United Kingdom national accounts : the blue book* (ONS), annual.

Many enquiry reports, not just Royal Commissions, remain parliamentary on the grounds that, if their recommendations are accepted, legislation will be required to implement them but some of the most important, such as the Beeching Report (*The reshaping of British Railways*, 2 vols., 1963) were departmental. More recently the First report of the Shipman Inquiry (*Death disguised*, 6 vols., 2002) was not parliamentary, but after complaints at the dearth of printed copies available, the Second and Third reports were published as Command Papers (2002–03 Cm 5853 and Cm 5854 respectively). There is no easy way to judge in advance whether such reports are or are not parliamentary and even those experienced in handling official publications know that it is necessary to check to discover this, especially if the library concerned keeps parliamentary papers separately or if the Command Paper number is required for ordering. A useful index from which to discover this is *British government publications : an index to chairmen and authors*. (4 vols.) London : Library Association, 1974–84 which covers the period 1801 to 1982. This indicates for each report whether it is parliamentary or not and gives its parliamentary citation or the name of the issuing department as appropriate. However the most important use for this series is to identify details of reports from the names of their chairmen or authors. Most reports are more usually known by these names but they seldom appear on the title-page, the 'Beeching Report' mentioned above being a case in point. In such cases many catalogues and indexes will omit the chairman's name. The Library Association's index is supplemented by annual HMSO/TSO lists. These are much less useful, not least because they are bulked out by the names of chairmen of Select Committees whose reports are never identified by their chairmen's names.

The first source for identifying British official publications should nowadays be electronic, notably **UKOP**, TSO's catalogue of UK official publications, in either its CD-ROM or online forms (see Chapter 8) but if this or other electronic sources are inaccessible or the material sought predates electronic coverage, the best general source is the TSO, formerly the HMSO, catalogues. These began in a modest way in 1836 as sessional sales catalogues of parliamentary papers (*List of parliamentary papers for sale*) and continued as such to 1893–94. Non-parliamentary papers ('official' publications in the terminology of the time) were first listed in a parallel annual catalogue from 1882 to 1893 (*List of official and parliamentary papers for exchange*). These were both superseded by the *Quarterly list ... of official and parliamentary papers for the year ...* for 1894 to 1896 after which this split into two series for official publications and parliamentary papers respectively. These quarterly lists were cumulative through the year so the fourth quarter was also an annual list.

From 1922 official (now called 'Stationery Office') publications and parliamentary papers were again combined in a single catalogue, now monthly but with the December issue cumulating the earlier issues as an annual called *Consolidated list of parliamentary and Stationery Office publications*, shortened in 1924 to *Consolidated list of government publications* or, in general usage, just the 'Consolidated List'. Thereafter there were a number of minor changes of title (particularly irritating in a catalogue) until it became the *Government publications catalogue* (again with variations) in 1954 and *HMSO annual catalogue* in 1985 (*The Stationery Office catalogue* from 1996). From 1936 the annual catalogue became separate with pagination spanning five years facilitating quinquennial indexes. Until then, the arrangement of official publications had been in broad subject groups identified by letters (e.g. 'Q' = Record publications, the publications of the Public Record Office). Generally each letter signified a single department but some were combined and there was a 'Miscellaneous' section, originally lettered 'R' but slipping to 'X' as new sections were introduced. Since then, non-parliamentary publications have been arranged alphabetically by issuing department and then by title; also the index, which had been non-existent before 1922 and poor afterwards, began to improve. Parliamentary and non-parliamentary publications have from the start been listed in separate sequences and the arrangement of the former has always been numerical by series. Since 1949 parliamentary papers have also been listed in the departmental sequence under the relevant department. In 1986 a third sequence was introduced listing Northern Ireland official publications (see Chapter 5). Previously these had been listed in a catalogue of publications issued separately by the Belfast office of HMSO.

The present repertoire of TSO catalogues now consists of a *Daily list* which contains everything put on sale by TSO the previous day including works for which it is the UK sales agent. This cumulates into a *Monthly catalogue* containing everything in that month's *Daily lists* except for SIs (see Chapter 1), including Northern Irish SRs and Scottish SSIs (see Chapter 5) for which there is a separate monthly and annual catalogue. Likewise the *Monthly catalogue* cumulates into an *Annual catalogue* which contains everything in that year's *Monthly catalogues* except the agency publications for which since 1955 there has been a separate catalogue. These agency publications contain a few publications of galleries or museums in Britain that undertake their own publishing but distribute through HMSO/TSO which have been included since 1936, but mostly consist of the sales publications of a wide range of IGOs (see Chapter 7), included since 1946.

Though extensive, this repertoire of catalogues is not comprehensive in its coverage of British government publications and the reason is a simple one – the catalogues were from the start *sales* catalogues and, though the term has long dropped out of its title, this remains the case. This has two implications. Firstly the catalogue ignores any publication that TSO or previously HMSO have issued free of charge – if its not sold, there's no listing. For example between 1967 and 1971 HMSO produced on behalf of the Decimal Currency Board a wide range of leaflets in vast quantities (some were distributed to every household in the land) but most were free and therefore did not figure in the HMSO catalogues at the time. Despite their quantity, these leaflets are now very hard to find or even identify. Secondly, neither HMSO nor TSO have ever had a monopoly of government publishing and, if a department chooses to use another publisher or publish a document itself, then it will not be listed by TSO, unless, of course, it is the sales agent for such a publication. Useful as they are these catalogues have to be supplemented by other sources.

Most government departments have issued lists of their own publications in the past, though fewer do so now. These vary widely in their scope and their utility but are broadly of two types. The first type is epitomised by *DTI publications in print* which listed everything in print whether or not it was new since the last issue while the other listed everything produced since the last issue whether or not it was still in print; an example was the National Assembly for Wales' [formerly the Welsh Office's] *Publications list for [year]*. It is indicative, however, that neither is still published in printed form. The same goes for an important catalogue produced by Chadwyck-Healey Ltd since 1980: *Catalogue of British official publications not published by HMSO* [later *TSO*] (6 issues per year with annual cumulations). This can now only be consulted in electronic form where it is combined with the HMSO/TSO catalogues to form **UKOP** (see Chapter 8).

There are a number of general guides to British official publications. Still the best, certainly the most comprehensive, is Rodgers (Frank) *A guide to British government publications*. New York : Wilson, 1980 which covers both parliamentary and non-parliamentary publications. The latter are examined department by department and for each is given the relevant statutes, administrative reports, statistical reports, serials, series, periodicals, regulations, non-serial publications, reports of committees, bibliographies and publications of subordinate and related bodies and agencies. Its age means that it is in need of updating but the same can be said of most other available guides. Of these should be mentioned Ollé (James G.) *An introduction to British government publications*, 2nd rev. ed. London : AAL, 1973; Pemberton (John E.) *British official publications*, 2nd rev. ed. Oxford : Pergamon, 1973; and Butcher (David) *Official publications in Britain*, 2nd ed. London : LA, 1991 which includes a rare chapter on local government.

Guides to sources rather than publications include Comfort (A. F.) and Loveless (C.) *Guide to government data : a survey of unpublished social science material in libraries of government departments in London*. London : BLPES, 1973; Picket (Kathleen G.) *Sources of official data*. [London] : Longman, 1974; and Richard (Stephen) *Directory of British official publications : a guide to sources,* 2nd ed. London : Mansell, 1984. Relatively up-to-date background information is available from Nurcombe (Valerie J.) (ed.) *Official publishing in the nineties.* London : SCOOP, 1998, the papers of two seminars. A welcome guide to a specialised source is *The guide to executive agencies.* Watford : Carlton, [1995–], usually annual. Also useful is TSO's annual *The Whitehall companion*; and there is the parallel *The local government companion* for local government. Part of the reason that few of the guides are recent is the increasing importance of electronic sources for official publications. For this reason, an important guide is Jellinek (Dan) *Official UK : the essential guide to government websites*, 2nd ed. London : TSO, 2000, although, because of the rapid developments in this area, this is already in need of revision.

There are also a number of more specialised guides, notably for statistics. One that is now useful only for historical purposes is an annual series that ran to 17 volumes between 1922 and 1938 called *Guide to current official statistics*. London : HMSO, 1923–1939. This was revived in 1976 as an irregular series under the title *Guide to official statistics*, with the latest edition being published by TSO for ONS in 2000. Another series issued jointly by the Royal Statistical Society and the Economic and Social Research Council is *Reviews of United Kingdom statistical sources* which was published (by three different publishers – Heinemann, Pergamon Press and Chapman & Hall) in 29 volumes between 1974 and 1993. Each volume is an in-depth study of the statistics of a particular topic though a few volumes combine separate monographs on different topics; Vol. III, for example, was on housing, Vol. XIV on rail transport and Vol. XX on religion. Good general guides are Mort (David) *UK statistics : a guide for business users.* [Aldershot] : Ashgate, 1992, and Levitas (Ruth) and Guy (Will) *Interpreting official statistics*. London & New York : Routledge, 1996. More specialised are Kerrison (Susan) and MacFarlane (Alison) *Official health statistics : an unofficial guide*. London : Arnold, 2000, and Fitches (Jan) and Grove (Isabel) (eds.) *SubNatStats 1999 : a subject index to sub-national statistics*. London : LRC, 1999, while an invaluable source for historical enquiries is Mitchell (B.R.) *British historical statistics*. Cambridge : Cambridge University Press, 1988.

Every government department and most subordinate bodies and government agencies have their own website on the internet and these rather than printed sources are the best guides to sources of relevant government information. Many of these sites contain bibliographic databases of their own publications and TSO especially through the UKOP database (available also as a CD-ROM) gives general access to British official publications. Increasingly, the internet gives access not just to records of publications but to the full texts of many of them as well. Chapter 8 gives more details.

Chapter 5.   Some special cases

The scope of official publishing is too extensive to be uniformly dealt with in depth in a monograph of this length but certain categories of official publications are more in demand than others. Based on the experience of the official publications staff at the Enquiry Desk of the Social Sciences Reading Room at the British Library, the following (all but the last topic) are what many enquirers are after or what they have difficulty in dealing with. The final topic (the publications of UK devolved governments) is included because it is, apart from the rather chequered history of Northern Ireland, comparatively new and probably, for most, uncharted territory.

Treaties

Treaties are international agreements between sovereign states. Sometimes only two states are involved and such treaties are described as bilateral and sometimes there are three or more in which case the treaty will be multilateral. A treaty need not necessarily be called a treaty; other terms used include agreement, pact, convention, protocol, exchange of notes or final act (in the last case, if the text of a treaty has been agreed at an international conference, the agreed version will be printed as the final act of the proceedings of the conference).

Not all international agreements or agreements involving states are treaties. An agreement between the government of a state and a body of its citizens (e.g. *Magna Carta*) is no treaty (see Chapter 1) and agreements between organisations not being governments are not treaties either; for example, an agreement between national library associations on the conditions for inter-library loans. Two famous treaties of the early twentieth century were, in fact, no such thing. The treaty of Vereeniging was actually the surrender document of the Boer forces in the South African War. As the Boer Republics had been annexed by Britain, there never was a peace treaty between them and the United Kingdom. The agreement which established the Irish Free State, now the Republic of Ireland, is commonly called simply 'The Treaty' in the Republic but the Free State which the agreement established could not, by definition, be a party to the agreement and in Britain it is more accurately called 'Articles of agreement for a treaty…'

Treaties in Britain have been issued in a numbered Treaty Series since 1892 and are identified as, for example, TS [or UKTS] 1974 no. 7. In addition, British treaties will also be issued as Command Papers, part of the parliamentary papers (see Chapter 3), and before the start of the treaty series this was the normal form of issue. In some instance a treaty will be officially published twice. Only ratified treaties are published in the Treaty Series and usually treaties are not published until ratification (this is why some treaties are only published several years after they were signed). Contrary to a widespread belief, parliament does not, indeed *cannot*, ratify treaties, unlike the senate in the United States, but some treaties require a change in the domestic law of the United Kingdom and this can usually only be effected by Parliament. In such circumstances the unratified treaty is published (as a Command Paper) so that Parliament has the necessary background information for the change in law. Once Parliament has passed the necessary legislation and the treaty has been ratified, it will be reissued (there is no difference in the text of a ratified and unratified treaty) in the Treaty Series.

The first source for finding treaties to which Britain is a party is *An Index to British treaties 1101–1968* published in 1970 in 3 volumes covering treaties up to the end of 1968. The treaties are listed in strict chronological order (day/month/year) and Vol. 1 contains indexes to bilateral treaties by country and by subject and to multilateral treaties by subject. Treaties are often known conventionally by where they were concluded, Treaty of Versailles, Berne Convention or Locarno Pact for example, but there is no place index although occasionally places are listed as subjects. A fourth volume was published in 1991 correcting and updating the first 3 volumes and covering the period 1969–1988. The entry for each treaty gives its title, the date and place of signature and ratification details (not just for Britain). It does not include any texts of treaties but does include sources for them. This usually means giving the UK Treaty Series number, the Command Paper number and the location in the bound set of parliamentary papers (see Chapter 3) but additional or alternative sources are given such as *British and Foreign State Papers* or *Rymer's Foedera*.

It also lists where appropriate a source for the text in the *League of Nations Treaty Series* (LNTS) or in the *United Nations Treaty Series* (UNTS). The UN, and the League of Nations before it, registers and reprints in their own 'treaty series' all the treaties concluded between member states. Nowadays that means virtually all treaties as even Switzerland is now a member of the UN. The usefulness of having a single source for the texts of virtually all treaties is obvious and the LNTS covers 1919 to 1945 and the UNTS from 1946. Clive Parry (the editor of *An index to British treaties*) was the principal editor for a series, the *Consolidated treaty series*, that attempted to reprint all the major international treaties from the Treaty of Westphalia in 1648, generally reckoned as the start of the modern diplomatic world, and the Treaty of Versailles in 1919 from when the LNTS takes over. Each of those three series, Parry's Treaties, LNTS and UNTS, has its own repertoire of indexes.

There is a class of treaty, once important but now virtually defunct, that gives special problems – where one party to an agreement is a nation-state in the modern sense but the other party is a tribal chiefdom not recognised as a 'country' by those who arrogantly claimed to be 'the Civilized World'. It was by means of such agreements that Britain and other European powers obtained much of their colonial empires and the United States spread westward at the expense of what were then called Indians (now 'native Americans') but they are often omitted in mainstream series of treaties. For Britain's colonial empire the best source for such treaties is *British and foreign state papers* where they are indexed under locality, tribe or chieftain. For Britain's Indian Empire (always considered quite distinct from the colonies), there is a special series, *A collection of treaties, engagements and sanads relating to India and neighbouring countries*, issued by the Government of India in 14 volumes in 1929. This not only includes agreements between the British authorities in India and the princely states there but also treaties concerning Tibet, Afghanistan, Persia (now Iran) and the Arab Sheikhdoms of the Gulf area.

Just as Britain maintains a *United Kingdom Treaty Series* (UKTS), so there are Treaty Series for most countries. These will be the primary sources for finding and seeing the texts of treaties of a given country in the country concerned but outside it there are often better, or at least easier, sources. If the UK is the other party to a bilateral treaty or one of the signatories to a multilateral one, the UKTS is likely to be the source sought. If the UK is not a party to the treaty concerned, the most appropriate source might well be the UNTS or for earlier periods (and with less certainty) 'Parry' or the LNTS.

For recent treaties, an online source is almost certainly likely to be the best source. There are often delays in publishing treaties. It may take time to ratify treaties and they are unlikely to be included in national treaty series or registered at the UN before ratification. In Britain some treaties are published before ratification for reasons explained above. Registration at the UN may be delayed, publication lags behind registration and the indexes lag behind publication. The Foreign and Commonwealth Office (FCO) Treaty Enquiry Service will advise on the status of treaties which involve the UK and its crown dependencies and overseas territories, and help with publication references. See **http://www. fco.gov.uk** for contact details and other information on treaties. Most government websites give access to treaties and there is a separate UN Treaties database (see Chapter 8).

Electoral registers

The Great Reform Act of 1832 (*Representation of the people act 1832* (2&3 Gul.4 cap.45)) is best known for abolishing the worst of the 'rotten boroughs' and increasing the franchise but among its reforms was the introduction of electoral registers. Before this anyone voting had to present himself at the place of the poll (only one per constituency), prove his right to vote and then cast it. The increase in the franchise but especially the reduction in the period of the poll from two weeks before 1828 to two days and later to a single day made it desirable to establish entitlement to vote in advance. Registers have been produced annually since then except for the two World Wars when none were produced and for a short period after the First World War (1919–26) when there were half-yearly registers.

Throughout the nineteenth century the extent of male franchise grew and in 1918 women over 30 gained the parliamentary vote, though they first appeared on the register nearly 40 years earlier when burgess rolls (registers of municipal voters) began to be merged with parliamentary registers. The ratepayer franchise for local government could include women from 1869, though at first only unmarried women. The franchise was equalised between the sexes in 1928 from when can be dated substantial universal adult suffrage. Increases in the franchise have been modest since then apart from the lowering of the voting age to 18 in 1969. After census returns, the electoral registers, even in the early days of a restricted franchise, are the largest listing of people in any given locality in Britain and are an invaluable source material for family research or local studies.

Census returns are unpublished and so are strictly out of the scope of this monograph but are often used in conjunction with electoral registers. Censuses have been taken every 10 years since 1801 but returns before 1841 do not survive and none are available after the 1901 returns which were released for public inspection in January 2002. The original enumerators' returns are too fragile for the heavy use that they would get so all the available returns for the censuses (1841–1901) have been filmed and the National Archives set of films can be consulted at the Family Records Centre. Most public libraries have acquired sets of films for those parts of the censuses relevant to their own areas. There is a name index for the 1881 census available on microfiche but not yet for the other censuses. Limited local name indexes compiled by family history societies exist and more extensive street indexes (the arrangement of the original returns is by enumeration district and then in a 'postman's-round' order following the route taken by the enumerator). The 1901 census returns have been issued online and when they were first made available the initial demand utterly swamped the system; it crashed and remained down for many months. It is freely searchable by name or address or by any element of the data recorded but there is a charge for access to the data that has been traced.

To revert to electoral registers, these contain the names of those entitled to vote. Until 1950, this meant those, otherwise qualified, who were 21 years of age on or after the qualifying date. From 1950 to 1968, it also included those (identified by a letter 'Y') who would have qualified for the next register if it had been half-yearly instead of annual who could vote on or after the date when that register would have taken effect (this was to compensate for the cancellation of half-yearly registers proposed in 1949 but immediately cancelled). From 1969, all otherwise qualified who were over 18 can be entered on the register; those attaining that age during the life of the register are entered with the date of their eighteenth birthday, from which date they can vote. The form in which names are currently given, with some latitude for oriental names, is surname followed by first forename and initial of the next forename, and any further forenames are suppressed. Earlier practice was more variable. Other information contained has also varied. It has always included place of abode, nowadays the full postal address. Until 1948 when there was more than one way to qualify to vote, the nature of the franchise was included either by code or by parallel listings. From the time that parliamentary registers began to serve as registers for other elections (currently European elections and sub-national elections for devolved governments and local authorities at every level), they indicate if someone is *not* entitled to vote in all elections. Formerly other information was included – absent or service voters were identified and those qualified for jury service. For a few years after the First World War, the separate absent voters lists included service details – rank, number and unit. From 1885 to 1915 registers showing the lodgers' franchise included the rent, the name of the landlord (or, more usually landlady) and details of the rooms rented.

Arrangement too has varied. Except for the period 1945–48, when they were derived from the National Register, registers have always been compiled locally, originally by parish. The parish overseer of the poor was responsible and the arrangement within parishes was alphabetical by voter. Parishes were normally arranged alphabetically within the constituency though other arrangements were possible. From 1878 it was permissible, later compulsory, to combine parliamentary and local authority registers. The latter were then essentially lists of rate-payers and, as rates were normally collected door-to-door, the registers were in street order and this pattern was extended to the combined registers. Currently registers for parliamentary constituencies are arranged by polling districts in alpha-numerical order of their codes. Within polling districts, the arrangement is by street in alphabetical order and then in street order. This does not mean in strict house-number order for, if a street numbers as 'odds and evens', the register will do the same and blocks of flats will have their residents listed as they occur in the street. In rural areas, where the word street is not a meaningful concept, the arrangement (within the smallest unit of local government, the parish or its equivalent) is alphabetical by voter and sometimes both arrangements will be found within the one register.

How to find electoral register information resolves itself into two separate questions – how to find the register for the right constituency and then how to locate a copy of it. The number, size and shape, and names of constituencies have been altered at irregular intervals, three times in the nineteenth century and six times in the twentieth. These have been effected by boundary commissions (*ad hoc* until 1918, permanent since 1948) and their reports and accompanying maps are the prime source for identifying the right constituency, supplemented by the legislation (acts of parliament or, more recently, statutory instruments) which put their recommendations into effect, sometimes with amendments until 1948. A number of alternative ways of tracking down the same information exist and these are explained in the introduction to Cheffins (Richard) *Parliamentary constituencies and their registers since 1832*. London : British Library, 1998, and in a free pamphlet issued by the British Library's Social Sciences and Official Publications department entitled *United Kingdom electoral registers*. A version of the pamphlet is available on the British Library website at **http://www.bl.uk/services/ information/spis_er.html**.

Locating copies of registers is not too difficult, although it has to be admitted that a surprising number of old registers no longer survive. The largest collection and the only nationwide collection permanently retained is held by the British Library whose set is complete from 1947. It also has some 20,000 earlier registers and its complete holdings are set out, with pressmarks, in *Parliamentary constituencies and their registers since 1832* mentioned above. The book also serves as a check-list of what registers have ever existed. Electoral registers are not subject to legal deposit and so the other Copyright Libraries do not have sets although the National Libraries of Scotland and Wales have substantially complete post-War sets for their respective countries. Apart from these the main sources outside the British Library are the county record offices for their respective counties and the larger city libraries for their own areas. A useful inventory of these holdings is Gibson (Jeremy) & Rogers (Colin) *Electoral registers since 1832*. 2nd ed. Birmingham : Federation of Family History Societies, 1990.

If it is the current or a recent issue of the electoral registers that is wanted, then there are other possibilities. Although the British Library is the only institution permanently to retain a complete set of registers, they are not available there during their year of currency but there is another institution that receives a complete set. This is the Social Survey Division of the Office for National Statistics and, unlike the British Library, their set is available for use within a few weeks of coming into force but it is retained only for two years. When that department was based at St Catherine's House in London, it was a very convenient source for those who wanted to consult recent registers, but they moved to Titchfield in Hampshire in 1995 and, although their set is still available to the public, this is much less convenient especially as staff are unable to check registers on behalf of remote enquirers. For more information telephone ONS directly: 01329-813074. For a few years ONS's two-year-old registers were passed to the Family Records Centre where they proved popular (perhaps because they were mistakenly perceived to be the current registers) but this has now ceased. Locally, current registers are normally available at public libraries or town halls (but see below).

The most important difference between recent registers and older ones is that the former are accessible electronically. Some months after the printed registers are published, they are available online via companies such as 192.com (**http:// www.192.com**) and its CD-ROM equivalent **UK–Info Disk** (see Chapter 8), and UKRoll (**http://www.ukroll.com/**). The advantage of any electronic search is not just its ease compared to manual searching but the fact that any element of the data can be used for searching. The printed register is address based and any search for a name without an address or at least a fairly precise locality is difficult, if not impossible. But a name search electronically is perfectly feasible although the number of people with identical names may surprise the enquirer.

There has, however, been a growing unease at the privacy and human rights implications of easy electronic name searching of registers. As a consequence, there have been major changes from the December 2002 register. The date of the register is the first change. With the introduction of continuous updating, the draft register has been abolished and the register proper now comes into force in December when the draft registers used to be issued and no longer in February as had been the case for nearly half a century. More importantly, registers will now be issued in two versions – a full version with restricted availability and an edited version available generally. The edited version omits any names of those who wish to be omitted and the form to complete for inclusion on the register has a box on it to indicate this preference. The full registers are still available to be consulted at the British Library, at the ONS and at local public libraries but no copying will be permitted and no downloading or data transfer will be permitted from an online version – 'handwritten notes' only will be permitted. Initial experience would seem to suggest that public libraries are reluctant to make the full registers available even under the new restrictions. The commercial suppliers of online versions of the register will, by law, have access *only* to the edited version. The effect of this is hard to judge. If only a few people opt out, the service will probably continue with a reduced coverage but if a major proportion of the electorate opt out, a service from commercial suppliers can hardly continue.

The *London gazette*

The *London gazette* is a newspaper; it was taxed as one when there was a newspaper stamp duty and it is registered as one at the Post Office for mailing purposes, but it is unlike any other newspaper. Its format is unlike other papers and has scarcely changed in nearly three and a half centuries, its original quarto size (normal for news-sheets at that time) being remarkably similar to its present A4 size. More importantly, it does not carry news, or not what mainstream newspapers would recognise as news. It is the organ for government announcements. Although this is well enough understood, there are sufficient misunderstandings to justify dealing with it separately.

The *London gazette* began life in 1665 as the *Oxford gazette* as the court had retreated to Oxford to avoid the plague in London but took its present title after a couple of dozen issues when the court returned. It was at first a weekly publication but soon became bi-weekly and then daily but the imposition of stamp duty made this uneconomic and it reverted to bi-weekly until well into the nineteenth century. It is now issued daily (five days a week) with numerous supplements which (with one exception) number with the main issues (both in issue numbers and page numbers). Page numbering began in 1785 and is continuous throughout the year, starting afresh at the beginning of each year. Indexes also began in 1785, half-yearly until the beginning of the twentieth century and quarterly since then. There are no cumulative indexes although there are instances of private indexes being produced (of bankruptcies, for example) that span many years.

The contents evolved slowly but have been relatively stable for centuries. First comes State Intelligence, containing a wide range of announcements, then two sections of awards (introduced in 1942 – they were formerly included in State Intelligence), a section on promotion and appointments, a section of advertisements and then several on bankruptcies. The index is organised in the same way. The *London gazette* is available online from 1998 (see Chapter 8).

Based on the experience at the British Library, by far the commonest use to which the *London gazette* is put is in connexion with gallantry and the other awards relating to war service. Provided the date is known searching for the award is not difficult but, if this is uncertain, the job is, at the least, tedious as four indexes have to be checked for each year. Until the end of 1941, the entry in the index was in the State Intelligence section under the award with names of recipients in alphabetical order. Gallantry and service awards (e.g. Military Cross or Distinguished Conduct Medal) are listed but not campaign medals (e.g. Africa Star) with a page reference (not date) against each name. Mentions in Despatches from the beginning of 1916 are entered under the service ministry (the Admiralty, War Office and, from the second quarter of 1918, the Air Ministry). Before that, all that is entered in the index are despatches themselves and no names are listed. Except for the earliest days (the system of mentioning in despatches began in India in the 1840s), names of those mentioned were not included *in* the despatches but in lists attached to them and later quite separately from the despatches. From 1942 the system of indexing changed. The various awards continued to be listed in the State Intelligence section but without names. These are to be found in two sequences following State Intelligence, one headed 'Honours, decorations and medals' and the other 'Mentions in despatches and Commendations' (King's or Queen's commendations were predominantly for civilians, for bravery *not* 'in the face of the enemy'). In each case, names are in a single alphabetical sequence without any indication of the award made. The *London gazette* website has an historical archive of all editions from 1914–1920 and 1939–1948, as well as all honours and awards in the twentieth century (see Chapter 8).

What is actually found in the body of the *London gazette* is often a sad disappointment. There is a widespread but mistaken belief that it carries a description, however brief, of the action or activity for which the award was made (what is called the citation). Citations are sometimes included but this is very much the exception overall, and for many awards (e.g. Mentions in despatches) the citation is *never* included and this is the case for any award, however exalted, gazetted (i.e. announced) in the half-yearly lists – the New Year's honours and the King's or Queen's Birthday honours lists. The purpose of gazetting awards is publicly to announce them and to provide legal evidence that the awards have been made, and anything more is, so to speak, a bonus. Foreign awards to British subjects are not, as such, gazetted. The ribbon, medal or decoration of a foreign award cannot be worn without permission and it is this permission to wear that is gazetted and indexed.

The Imperial War Museum (IWM) has produced a series of information leaflets which are invaluable in identifying what is available (and where) so far as medals are concerned (and for service records as well but this does not involve the *London gazette*). There are separate leaflets for the Army, the Royal Navy, Royal Marines and the Women's Royal Naval Service, the Royal Air Force, the Household Cavalry and Guards Division, the Merchant Navy, Prisoner of war records (all services), Queen Mary's Army Auxiliary Corps, Voluntary Aid Detachments, and for the Auxiliary Territorial Service. Versions of some of these leaflets are available on the family history pages of the IWM website at **http://www.iwm.org.uk/lambeth/famhist.htm** while four were expanded into short books published by the IWM in 1999–2000 entitled *Tracing your family history: Army* (the others are *Royal Air Force*, *Royal Navy* and *Merchant Navy*). More detailed information on specific decorations can be found in Abbott (P.E.) & Tamplin (J.M.A.) *British gallantry awards*. London : Nimrod Dix, 1981.

Mention was made that there was one exception to supplements being numbered in sequence with the regular issues. This is the Premium Bond supplements, about half a dozen a year. These are much larger than an average issue and are often around 1,000 pages long. They consist exclusively of premium bond numbers, current winning numbers and unclaimed prize numbers from before, 96 numbers to a column, eight columns to a page, perhaps 750,000 numbers to an issue.

From the earliest days, the *London gazette* has been a useful source for tracing bankruptcies. The information available has varied over time, sometimes details of the bankruptcies themselves and discharges from bankruptcy, at other times notices of calling of creditors' meetings and such like. Bankruptcy involves people and not companies and it is information about personal bankruptcies that are recorded in the *London gazette*. Companies become insolvent, call in the receiver, are put into administration, are wound up or dissolved but do not become bankrupt. Details of company insolvencies and related matters and also of the formation of new companies can be found in the Companies supplement to the *London gazette* which is not a supplement like the others but essentially a separate publication – *London gazette : company law official notifications* (1973–) in microfiche.

To revert to the *London gazette* proper, it is also used to trace changes of name. It is true that the advertisement of changes of name can be given in the *London gazette* but, contrary to popular belief, it is neither the only nor even the principal way of doing so. Leaving aside name changes at marriage, there are some half-dozen ways of changing one's name. The simplest is just to announce the change to your friends and give your bank manager a new signature. More formally, and the most common way, is by deed poll – swearing an oath to this effect before a commissioner of oaths. This is sufficient on its own but deeds can also be registered at the High Court or, if a coat of arms is changed at the same time, at the College of Arms. The change can at the same time be publicly announced, in local or national papers and, of course, in the *London gazette*. Finally it is theoretically possibly to change one's name by royal licence or by a private act of parliament (see Chapter 1). This has not been done for nearly a century, and that an isolated case, and it would surely no longer be permitted. For more information on this subject see *Change of name*. 15th ed., edited by Helen Mead, London : FT Law & Tax, 1995 or Pearce (Nasreen) *Change of name : the law and practice*. London : Callow, 2003.

Devolved governments

The United Kingdom is the result of the merger of four component countries over a long period of time. First in 1284, England and Wales were united or, to be more accurate, after Edward I's conquest of the Principality, England annexed Wales and, in 1536, its independent legal system was abolished. In 1707, after more than a century of personal union under the Stuarts, England and Scotland were united as Great Britain by acts of both their parliaments. Scotland retained a separate legal system and national church. Ireland's Parliament had been subordinated to that of England in the fifteenth century and in 1801 Ireland and Great Britain were united. In the twentieth century this process has to a greater or lesser extent been put into reverse with important consequences for official publications.

From the start of the Irish Union there was a strong and sometimes violent opposition to it. This was generally called the 'Home Rule' campaign (the term then used for devolution) though many campaigners fought for independence and eventually achieved it for the greater part of the island. The irony was that most of Ulster which was most opposed to Home Rule was, in the end, the only part to achieve it. The *Government of Ireland act 1920* (10&11 Geo 5 cap. 67) established devolved parliaments for Southern Ireland and Northern Ireland but the provisions were a dead letter for the South. A Northern Ireland Parliament and government was, however, established in 1921. It was, both in its organisation and its publications, a miniature Westminster. Parliament had two Houses, the House of Commons and the Senate and the government was formed from the major party in the House of Commons (throughout its whole life, the Ulster Unionist Party). Its legislation consisted of acts of parliament (public and general, local and personal, and private) and statutory rules and orders. Its parliamentary publications consisted of *Parliamentary debates* (*Hansard*) of both Houses, *Journals* of both Houses, business papers, and parliamentary papers, bills, House of Commons papers (and Senate papers from 1956) and Command papers. These last were prefixed 'Cmd' like their then United Kingdom equivalent at the time and like them they numbered consecutively through sessions. Unlike their UK equivalent, the Northern Ireland House of Commons Papers (and Senate papers) also numbered consecutively through sessions. Outside Parliament there were Northern Ireland government departments and they too issued their own publications. Virtually all Northern Irish official publications, statutory, parliamentary or departmental were issued by the Belfast branch of HMSO.

The Northern Ireland Parliament was prorogued in 1972 and dissolved the following year and most of the parliamentary publications ceased then: the *Votes*, the *Journals*, *Hansard* and the House of Commons and Senate papers. Command Papers which originate outside Parliament continued for a while but petered out in 1975 for want of an institution to present them to. *Statutory rules and orders* continued though renamed *Statutory rules* but 'Acts of Parliament' ceased. Primary legislation, however, continued in the form of (British) orders–in–Council passed under the authority of the *Northern Ireland act 1974* (1974 cap. 28) and some transitional legislation before that. The annual volumes of these orders–in–Council continued to bear the spine title of 'Northern Ireland Statutes' and when annual volumes ceased to be issued (after 1980), the ring binders issued as permanent holders for the individual Orders had the same spine title. Departmental publications continued as before and some papers which would have been issued as House of Commons Papers or Command Papers were now issued in this form.

The British Government was keen to restore a devolved government to Northern Ireland and an Assembly was elected to succeed the defunct Parliament in 1973 and a cross-party executive took office in January 1974 but lasted only until May that year though the Assembly was not formally dissolved until April 1975. This short-lived Assembly issued its own *Journals* and *Official report* (*Hansard*) and issued its series of Papers: Northern Ireland Assembly Papers (NIA 1-). It was a true legislature and its primary legislation was called 'Measures' and bills were called 'Draft Measures' through only three were passed before the Assembly collapsed. Departmental publications and *Statutory rules* continued. Another Northern Ireland Assembly was established but it was not a legislature (it was set up with the job of scrutinising the work of the government of the province and to devise a scheme of devolution) and there was no executive (at least none answerable to it). It produced its own Hansard and Northern Ireland Assembly Papers and in both cases, it was reckoned to be a continuation of the previous Assembly with its Hansard starting at Vol. 4 and its papers at NIA 30.

Under the terms of the *Belfast agreement* (1997–98 Cm 3883), popularly known as the Good Friday Agreement, a third Northern Ireland Assembly was established. Elections were held in June 1998 and the Assembly met in July. The cross-party Executive took longer to form but did eventually take office in December 1999. At this point, the New Northern Ireland Assembly, so-called, dropped the 'New' and was from then regarded as a continuation of the previous two Assemblies. In the interim its papers were designated NNIA 1-, since then as NIA [year] 1-. Legislation is in the form of Acts and, in draft form, as 'Bills' and *Hansard* has been resumed. Although devolution has been achieved for Northern Ireland, its success is precarious. The (third) Northern Ireland Assembly has already been suspended on more than one occasion in its short life and its continuation is far from assured. As a consequence, it is far from clear whether those publications arising directly from the Assembly, *Hansard*, NIA papers, Northern Ireland Acts, etc., will continue but whatever the case, administrative devolution will continue and departmental publications will still be issued together with *Statutory rules* and some form of primary legislation for Northern Ireland.

After the convolutions of devolution in Northern Ireland, the situation in Scotland and Wales is much simpler but also different, not only from Northern Ireland, but from each other. Devolution was proposed for both countries in 1978 but was decisively rejected in Wales while in Scotland though a majority were in favour in a referendum, the total vote did not reach the necessary threshold. Twenty years later the result was very different, a small majority in favour in Wales (albeit on a low turnout) and a decisive majority in Scotland. As a result a Scottish legislative Parliament and executive and a Welsh Assembly were established in 1998. The latter is a deliberative body and not a legislature; it also took over the administrative role of the Welsh Office which was merged with it.

In Scotland, the Parliament was empowered to pass Acts (Acts of the Scottish Parliament or ASPs) issued with *Explanatory notes* and to approve Scottish Statutory Instruments (SSIs) made under the authority of ASPs and these too sometimes have *Explanatory notes*. There is a full panoply of parliamentary papers – *Business Bulletin* (the equivalent of Westminster's Vote Bundle), Official report (*Hansard*) in several series (Plenary, Written Answers Report (WAR), Committees) in a 'daily' form (or as often as there is a sitting) and in a permanent bound form for the Plenary report, issued monthly and incorporating WARs and an index.

Committee reports are issued, that is reports of Committees of enquiry and bound volumes (one for each committee) with indexes are also issued. In addition there are *Minutes of proceedings* of the plenary sessions recording decisions taken and *Minutes of proceedings in committee* available online but not printed separately but included in the bound volumes of *Committee reports*. Draft legislation is issued in the form of bills with separate series of Executive bills ('government' bills), Members' bills and private bills. Bills amended are reprinted as amended and marshalled lists of amendments are issued. Series of *Explanatory notes* and *Policy memoranda* are issued for Executive bills and *Financial memoranda* for Members' bills. Finally there is issued something called 'Passage of bills' which includes each printing of a bill, explanatory notes, official reports on the bill, amendments and any other relevant documents.

The Scottish Executive took over from the Scottish Office on devolution and its publications ('laid papers') are issued in a numbered SE series. Although they are treated as parliamentary, the *Explanatory notes* to bills and acts and the *Policy memoranda* and *Financial memoranda* are generated from the Executive and not Parliament and other memoranda are issued as Executive publications. For both Parliamentary and Executive publications, the primary output is online via the internet (see Chapter 8) but, unlike Wales, everything, with minor exceptions is also issued in print form.

Devolution in Wales is distinctive in several ways. Firstly the National Assembly for Wales is not a legislature. There are no 'Welsh Acts of Parliament' though the Parliament of the United Kingdom can and occasionally does pass acts specifically for Wales. There *are* Welsh Statutory Instruments but these are British SIs numbered as such and approved by the UK Parliament but they also have a separate 'W' numbering and are drafted by the Welsh National Assembly (as they were formerly drafted by the Welsh Office) and they will in future be omitted from the annual bound volumes of SIs and be issued in a parallel series of Welsh

SIs. Secondly, unlike Scotland and Northern Ireland or indeed the UK as a whole, there is not the same distinction between the legislature and the executive or between parliamentary and non-parliamentary (executive) publications. On devolution the former Welsh Office became part of the Welsh National Assembly and became its secretariat.

But two other factors are most distinctive insofar as publishing is concerned. Wales is a bilingual country despite the fact that most who live there are monoglot English speakers and its published output is largely bilingual. Its parliamentary debates have the text in two columns; on the left is a substantially verbatim report in the language delivered of speakers in the Assembly (in English or Welsh as the case may be) and on the right a translation (except that in the overnight version only a Welsh to English translation is provided). Other publications are also bilingual though usually with one text following the other rather than in parallel columns. The most controversial distinction, however, was the decision to publish exclusively in the electronic format only, making its publications available on the Internet (continuations of Welsh Office publications and new executive-type publications are issued in print form and appear in an annual list). The Scottish Parliament and Executive and the (New) Northern Ireland Assembly also issue their publications on the Internet but they also publish in print form. The only paper publications of the National Assembly for Wales are printouts from the online texts. A copy of these are deposited in each 'Link Library' (one per constituency in Wales) and a copy in each of the legal deposit (Copyright) Libraries.

The main output of the Assembly is the *Official record* (*Hansard*), the overnight version simply called the *Record*, with a separate series for the plenary sessions and for written answers, committee documents, their papers and minutes, standing orders and laid papers. The output of the former Welsh Office, hitherto 'British' non-parliamentary papers, continues as National Assembly for Wales publications. A few of these (inspection reports of TECs (Technical & Enterprise Councils) for example) have converted to electronic only format but most continue unchanged with the change of issuing body hardly noticeable.

Although political devolution, even for Northern Ireland, is comparatively recent, administrative devolution has a longer history. Throughout the period of the Union, Ireland had a high degree of administrative devolution with its own administration in Dublin under a Chief Secretary and its own government departments and civil service. When devolution was suspended in Northern Ireland a separate administration was preserved for the Province answerable to a Secretary of State for Northern Ireland. Scotland on its union with England retained its own church and judicial system but as this was by treaty, it cannot be called devolution and it has little relevance to publications. Administrative devolution began in the late nineteenth century for Scotland. A Secretary for Scotland was appointed in 1885 with cabinet rank in 1892, becoming a Secretary of State in 1926. Within the Scottish Office, separate government departments evolved as for Agriculture or for Education. A similar evolution occurred for Wales though later and more slowly. A Minister for Welsh Affairs was appointed in 1951 but the post was held jointly by the Home Secretary until 1957 and the Minister for Housing and Local Government until 1964 when a separate Secretary of State for Wales was appointed and a Welsh Office established. On (political) devolution the publications of these Offices and their departments became publications of the Scottish Executive and National Assembly for Wales respectively.

The best guide to the publications of devolved governments of the UK is *Parliaments and Assemblies of the British Isles* edited by Valerie J. Nurcombe issued by SCOOP (the Standing Committee on Official Publications) and published by the Library Association in 2000. This also covers parliamentary publications of the Irish Republic, the Isle of Man and the various Channel Islands. For Northern Ireland for the period of its Parliament there is: Maltby (A) *The government of Northern Ireland 1922–1972 : a catalogue and breviate of Parliamentary Papers*. Dublin : IUP, 1974. From 1921 to 1986, HMSO Belfast issued its own monthly catalogue with cumulations. Since then Northern Irish official publications have been included in the HMSO (now TSO) Daily lists and Monthly and Annual catalogues where they form a separate sequence. Statutory rules are included in the monthly and annual lists of Statutory Instruments. The second Assembly is covered by O'Leary (C.) [et al.] *The Northern Ireland Assembly 1982–1986 : a constitutional experiment*. London : Hurst, 1988. For legislation, particularly for the direct rule period, there is: *Northern Ireland legislation* (House of Commons Information Office. Factsheet L8); also G. Woodman's 'Legislation in Northern Ireland' in: *The Law Librarian*, Aug. 1987. Also of value is the same author's 'Northern Ireland' in: Winterton (J.) & Moys (E. M.) *Information sources in law*. 2nd ed. London : Bowker Saur, 1997.

Already some useful guides have been published on the devolved governments in Wales and Scotland in addition to the SCOOP publication mentioned above. For Scotland there is Moore (John) and Munro (Kay) *Scottish official publications : an introduction and guide*. Edinburgh : TSO, 2001. A useful work that covers the UK and European Parliaments as well as the Scottish Parliament is Convery (Jane) *The Governance of Scotland : a Saltire guide*. 2nd ed. Edinburgh : TSO, 2001. This is updated by supplements and there is a linked subscription only website at **http://www.saltireguide.co.uk/**

For the Scottish Parliament an invaluable weekly guide (with six-monthly indexes) to its publications and business and information about it is WHISP

(*What's happening in the Scottish Parliament*), the Scottish equivalent of the *Weekly information bulletin* (see Chapter 3). There is nothing comparable for Wales but there is a useful recent guide to Welsh sources in *The Directory of Welsh government, 2003*. Watford : Carlton, [2002]. The Welsh Office for many years had published an annual catalogue of its publications and this continues (now online) under its metamorphosis to the National Assembly for Wales. TSO continues to publish most publications of the Scottish Parliament and Executive and these are included in its repertoire of catalogues, daily, monthly and annual in print form and online. As all three devolved administrations are heavily committed to online access, the best way to discover what exists and to view the text of their publications is to visit their respective websites (see Chapter 8).

Chapter 6. Foreign official publications

The wide range of official publications issued by the British government both historically and at present as outlined in the preceding chapters can be replicated by the publishing of governments abroad. There are some 191 countries that are members of the United Nations Organisation and with the accession of Switzerland in 2002 this now includes virtually all sovereign states (only the Vatican and some disputed territories – Palestine, Northern Cyprus and the Western Sahara – are excluded). A significant number of these are federal states where the component states or provinces within their own competence under the constitution are equally sovereign with the federal government. By contrast the devolved governments within the United Kingdom are, in constitutional terms, glorified units of local government, established by central government and capable equally of being abolished by central government (as the recent history of devolution in Northern Ireland shows). But it is not just sovereign states that have official publications – dependent territories (what were formerly known as colonies) have them too and the publications of inter-governmental organisations are also official. The latter publications will be dealt with in the next chapter. Here the publications of foreign governments, sovereign and dependent, federal and provincial are considered. The output in aggregate is vast and cannot possibly be dealt with in a brief chapter. Instead the range of publications produced is indicated by a few examples taken from diverse sources.

One type of publication that almost all other countries have but which is absent in Britain is a Constitution. This is not to say that the United Kingdom lacks a constitution as is frequently stated but that it is not contained in a single document called 'The Constitution' (with a capital 'C'). Instead it is embodied in a range of laws on constitutional matters and unwritten conventions. Elsewhere the norm is a written constitution, and New Zealand and Israel are the only considerable countries to have followed the British practice. The trend was set by the United States where a constitution was essential, as in all federal states, to define how the sovereignty shared between the federal and state governments was to be divided. The first American constitution, the Articles of Confederation proved inadequate and the present constitution, adopted in 1789 is now the oldest still in force in the world. Constitutions are laws, albeit very special laws often with different, more stringent, methods of being altered, and the text will often be found at the beginning of the collections of laws for the country as well as being widely available as separate documents. A number of websites act as gateways to constitutions online (see Chapter 8).

For most Commonwealth countries (Mozambique and Cameroon being the main exceptions) a prime source for their initial constitution, the 'Independence

Constitution', is to be found in *British* legislation. At first this was effected by (British) acts of parliaments. Thus the Canadian Constitution was embodied in the *British North America act 1867* (30 Vic. cap.3) and even amendments were enacted at the request of Canadian governments by further amending *British North America acts*. In 1982 the Canadian Constitution was patriated and renamed (in Canada) as the *Constitution act* and subsequent amendments have been within the competence of Canada to enact. More usually independence constitutions have been passed, not by acts of parliaments but by subordinate legislation. The relevant 'Independence Act' is simply concerned with severing Britain's authority over the territory and an 'Independence Order' is also passed as an order-in-Council issued as a statutory instrument, the schedule to which contains the independence constitution for the territory. Within the territory the text of the new constitution would be issued in its government gazette and any subsequent amendment or any new constitutions that replace the 'Independence Constitution' can only be found there or elsewhere in the territory concerned.

Thus the Independence Constitution for Malta can be found as a schedule to the *Malta independence order 1964* (SI 1964 No. 1398) and in the *Malta government gazette* No. 11,688 of September 18, 1964. The current constitution (the Independence Constitution as amended) can be found in Vol.1 of *The revised edition of the laws of Malta in force, 1985–* now continuously updated. It is also published as a separate pamphlet by the Government of Malta. But for most people (outside Malta) the best source for the text is a commercial encyclopaedia: *Constitutions of the countries of the world*. Dobbs Ferry, NY : Oceana, 1971– . 20 vols., looseleaf. This is comprehensive in scope, constantly revised and for non-English speaking countries (or, to be more accurate, where English is not an official language) the text of the constitution is given in an official language with an accurate but obviously unofficial English translation. It covers sovereign states but is supplemented by *Constitutions of dependencies and special sovereignties*. (From 1998 entitled *Constitutions of dependencies and territories*) Dobbs Ferry : NY, Oceana, 1975– . 7 vols., looseleaf.

Another category of official publications absent in the British system but widespread, though far from universal, elsewhere is that of law codes. The legal systems of most states in the world fall into two categories. England, the United States and most of the Commonwealth have a Common Law system of jurisprudence, whereas the countries of continental Europe and their former colonies have a Civil Law, or Roman Law, system. The French legal system was thoroughly revised by Napoleon and most other Roman law countries have revised their legal systems along very similar lines, particularly in the matter of codes of law (an important exception is Scotland, a Roman law country that has never adopted Napoleonic-style codes). There are generally five codes: a civil code, a criminal code, a code of civil procedure, a code of criminal procedure, and a commercial code but other codes are possible. Codes are laws and will be found in the relevant collections of laws such as the *Raccolta ufficiale delle leggi* ... in Italy; they will also be issued separately both by the government and by commercial publishers such as Dalloz in France. Some of the commercially published codes are conveniently in English translation such as the *Civil code of the Russian Federation* ... London & Moscow : White & Case, 1995 or the *French code of criminal procedure* ... Rev. ed. Littleton, Colo : Rothman, 1988. This is No.29 in an extensive series of codes in English, the 'American series of foreign penal codes' which are now available via the publisher W. S. Hein.

Although not a Roman Law country, the United States has a form of codified law, *The United States code* (USC). This comprises the whole extant statute law of the Federal state (it excludes any laws of individual states) rearranged in some 50 subject sections called 'Titles'. The work is massive in size, the index alone exceeding 8,000 pages and in this respect it is very different from the Napoleonic codes of other countries. It is issued in a new edition every 6 years and 2000 is currently the latest edition. There are annual supplements in the intervals between editions. There is a second code produced by the US government which is even less like the codes of other countries. The subordinate legislation of the United States, the equivalent of British statutory instruments, are collectively known as 'Federal Regulations' and these are gathered together (those in force) in a *Code of federal regulations* (CFR). Like the USC, the contents of the CFR are rearranged in Titles, which however do not necessarily correspond to the Titles of the USC. The CFR is issued annually but not all at one go. Roughly the first third of Titles are published in January each year, the next third in April and the remainder in September so that, for any particular title, the interval between one edition and the next is 12 months. It has its own extensive index.

For the rest, most types of the official publications found in Britain will have their parallels elsewhere, though always with national variations. Thus each country will have a set of enacted legislation and executive orders, government gazettes, legislative debates, papers laid before the legislature and a wide range of information papers issued by the executive and its agencies. A few examples chosen from different countries will suffice.

The *London gazette* may be among the oldest of government gazettes (the *Gaceta de Madrid* is even older, dating from 1661) but it is, in one important respect, not typical. In almost all other countries, including those formerly administered by Britain, it is the normal practice to promulgate laws by publishing them first in their official gazettes. Indeed, in most cases, such laws do not come into effect until they have appeared in the gazette (usually a fixed number of days later, reflecting the slower communications of the period when the system began). Gazettes take many different titles in different countries – 'Government ...' or

'Official …' Gazette or Journal or Bulletin or Monitor. It is difficult to identify particular gazettes unless the library you are using lists its holdings by country rather than by title. Lists of gazettes therefore are useful. One such is *Government gazettes: an annotated list of gazettes held* … New York : Dag Hammarskjöld Library, 1964. Many new countries have sprung up since then but for the countries already in existence, the list is still useful as gazettes are fairly stable in both title and content. More recent is Roberts (John E.) *A guide to official gazettes and their contents*, Rev. ed. Washington, DC : Law Lib., Lib. of Congress, 1985.

Gazettes elsewhere, as the primary source for the country's laws, have a much more important place in the output of official publications than does the *London gazette* in the UK and nowhere is this more so than in France. There, the present gazette started in 1869 (there had been earlier gazettes) as the *Journal officiel de l'Empire français* and, following the establishment of the Third Republic the following year, became the *Journal officiel de la Republique française* which, apart from the troubled period of the Second World War, has remained its title. It began as a single series, principally concerned with promulgating laws but gradually it expanded and split into numerous different series and many documents that would elsewhere be published separately from the gazette constitute a series of the *Journal officiel* in France. There are four main series, all daily: *Lois et Décrets* (Laws and Decrees), *Débats parlementaires* (Parliamentary Debates, in separate series for the National Assembly and for the Senate, the two Houses of the French Parliament), *Avis et rapports du Conseil Economique et Social* (Opinions and Reports of the Economic and Social Council) and *Documents administratifs* (Administrative documents) and dozens of lesser ones.

Statute law in addition to being first promulgated in the official gazette is generally reissued in its own series. In Italy for example, they appear first in the *Gazzetta ufficiale della Repubblica italiana* (Official gazette of the Italian Republic) but are then reissued in the *Raccolta ufficiale delle leggi dei decreti della Repubblica italiana* (Official compilation of the laws and decrees of the Italian Republic) which, as the name suggests, also includes subordinate legislation (*decreti* or decrees). In Germany there are two gazettes, one exclusively for laws (including treaties), the *Bundesgesetzblatt* (Federal law gazette), and a general gazette, the *Bundesanzeiger* (Federal gazette).

Parliamentary proceedings may be published as part of the gazette in France but it is more usually published as a distinct series, or several series, usually under the auspices of the legislature itself. Typical is the Dutch situation. The *Verslag van de Handelingen der Eerste en Tweede Kamer* (Proceedings of the First and Second Chambers) is principally the verbatim report of both chambers of the Dutch parliament including oral questions but there is much else contained in it – proceedings of joint sittings and of committees, appendices of answers to written questions, and various supplements of parliamentary papers. The situation in Germany is similar, if rather more elaborate. There are separate series for the two Houses of the German Parliament: the *Verhandlungen des Bundesrates* (Proceedings of the Federal Council – the upper chamber where the Länder or provinces are represented) and the *Verhandlungen des deutschen Bundestages* (Proceedings of the German Federal Assembly – the lower, popularly elected, chamber). Each proceedings has two sub-series: *Stenographische Berichte* (Stenographic reports, containing debates, resolutions and questions) and *Drucksachen* (Documents, for the Bundesrat) or *Anlagen zu den stenographischen Berichten* (Appendices to the stenographic reports, for the Bundestag) which contain documents including draft laws, enquiries, reports, motions and EU proposals. Chronologically, the *Verhandlungen* are organised into Wahlperioden (electoral periods or Parliaments) and volumes number within them. An index, *Register zu den Verhandlungen des deutschen Bundestages und des Bundesrates* (Index to the Proceedings of the German Federal Assembly and the Federal Council) cumulates annually and consists of a subject and a name index to all parts of the proceedings. It is not uncommon for parliamentary papers to be closely associated with parliamentary proceedings in this way. In Canada, Australia and South Africa, parliamentary papers are effectively annexes to their *Votes and proceedings*, the daily business papers of parliament.

The US equivalent of the parliamentary papers is the Congressional Serial Set though the parallel is far from exact. Like the parliamentary papers, this is not a reprint of the documents that it contains but a gathering of them in a prescribed order. It contains Congressional *Journals*, administrative reports, Congressional reports on legislation, reports of Congressional Committees, annual reports of Federal executive agencies, some statistical series and a variety of other reports and papers. The system was devised in 1895 and applied retrospectively back to 1817. Earlier papers (1789–1838) of a similar character had previously been reissued in a series called *American state papers* arranged in broad subject groups. Currently the Serial Set is organised in four series, House of Representatives ('House') Reports and Documents and Senate Reports and Documents; formerly there were additional series, e.g. House Executive Documents or Senate Miscellaneous Documents. Individual documents are identified by the Congress and Session, Series and document number, e.g. 32nd Congress, 2nd Session, House Report No. 35 (32-2 HR 35). Congressional Committee reports are part of the Congressional Serial Set but the rest of their publications are not. These most important documents are issued separately and comprise Hearings or transcripts of the Committee's interrogation of witnesses (similar in character to the Royal Commissions' proceedings) and Committee Prints, the written evidence, commissioned reports and miscellaneous papers of the Committee. Congressional hearings and committee prints from the 1830s have been reissued in microfiche by the Congressional Information Service (CIS) and the CIS indexes to this set provide an excellent bibliography to this material.

The range of the foreign equivalent to non-parliamentary publications can only be hinted at by a few examples – *The Philippine statistical yearbook*, 1977– . Manila : Nat. Economic and Development Authority; *Presupuesto de egresos de la Federación: proyecto*, Mexico : Secretaria de Programacion y Presupuesto, 1937– . (Budget expenditures of the Federal Government : draft); *Showa 60-Nen Kokusei Chosa Hokoku/1985 National population census.* Tokyo : Tokeikyoku/Statistics Bureau, 1986– ; *Civil list of the Indian Administrative Service.* New Delhi : Dept. of Personnel and Training, irregular; *The New Zealand education gazette*, 1921– , Wellington : Min. of Education; *Déclarations* ([Presidential] statements), Paris : Documentation française, 1974– , weekly; *Annual report.* Tripoli : Central Bank of Libya; and *Labour market and labour market policy.* Copenhagen : Ministry of Labour, annual (an official English translation of the Ministry's report to Parliament).

Many countries publish specific bibliographies of official publications such as *Government publications in Finland/Valtion virallisjulkaisut/Statens officiella publikationer, 1961– .* Helsinki : Eduskunnan kirjasto; *Chongbu kanhaengmul mongnok* (Government publications list), 1948/65– . Seoul : Chongbul Kanhaengbul Jaejakso, annual; *Monthly catalog of United States government publications, 1940– .* Washington, DC : US Govt. Printing Office (earlier publications are covered by *Checklist of United States public documents, 1789–1909* and *Catalogue of public documents*, 1893–1940); and *Sdu catalogues* (catalogue of the State Printer and Publisher). Den Haag : Staatsdrukkerij en Uitgeverij (Sdu), annual. Official publications can also be found in national bibliographies and, in the absence of official publications catalogues, are likely to be the only source for them. *Malawi national bibliography : list of publications deposited in the Library of the National Archives.* Zomba, 1967– , irregular, is a case in point. In some instances, exterior sources are likely to be the most convenient or even the only source, for example the *Accessions list : eastern and southern Africa.* Nairobi : US Library of Congress Office, 1993– , bi-monthly with annual serials supplement and annual publishers directory which covers 23 countries and is not confined to official publications. More universal in scope is the *Bibliographic guide to government publications – foreign.* Boston : G.K. Hall, annual, which is based upon the extensive collections of the New York Public Library and the Library of Congress and is paralleled by the *Bibliographic guide to government publications – US.* Much older but still of value historically is *List of serial publications of foreign governments, 1815–1931*, edited by Winifred Gregory. New York : H.W. Wilson, 1932. From a British perspective it should be understood that 'foreign' in the context of an American publication will include Britain and exclude the United States.

There is a wide range of guides to official publications in many countries. Examples are: *La documentation administrative* (government documentation). Paris : Ministère de l'Education Nationale, de la Jeunesse et des Sports, 1988; *Guide de l'accès aux documents administratifs* (Guide to access to government documents). Paris : Commission d'Acces aux Documents Administratifs, 1992 and *Clé des sources* (Key to [statistical] sources). Paris : INSEE, 1992– in France and similar publications elsewhere. External, multinational guides like Porgès (Laurence) *Sources d'information sur l'Afrique noire francophone et Madagascar* (sources for information on French-speaking Black Africa and Madagascar). Paris : Ministère de la Coopération, 1988 are invaluable in filling some gaps in national coverage. Multi-national guides are rarer; three that are particularly useful are *Official publications of western Europe*, edited by Eve Johansson, 2 vols. London & New York : Mansell, 1984–88, which, as the title suggests is regional in scope, the *Guide to official publications of foreign countries*, 2nd ed. [Chicago] : American Library Association, Government Documents Round Table, [1997] which covers every country in the world with a population over 100,000 except, of course, the United States itself, and *Information sources in official publications*, edited by Valerie Nurcombe. London : Bowker-Saur, 1997.

Again the best access to foreign official publications is now the Internet. There are a number of gateways to official publications or to law or legislation and there are others directing you to national websites. The main ones currently available are noted in Chapter 8. It is hardly surprising that the largest and richest collections of official publications cover the United States. For these there are a number of useful printed guides including *Government information on the Internet*, 6th ed., edited by Peggy Garvin. Lanham, Md. : Bernan, 2003.

Chapter 7.   Publications of inter-governmental organisations

The number of international organisations is vast. Volume I of the 2002–03 edition of the *Yearbook of international organizations*, which lists such organisations in a single alphabetical sequence, contains 25,542 entries and, although the bulk of them are for NGOs (see the Introduction), the numbers of IGOs must still run to thousands. A rare general guide to the published output of IGOs (as opposed to that of individual organisations) is *International information, documents, publications and electronic information of international organizations*, 2nd ed., edited by Peter I. Hajnal, 2 vols. Englewood, Colo. : Libraries Unlimited, 1997–2001. For convenience I have grouped IGOs in three. Firstly the United Nations itself, then its agencies, Unesco, the FAO, etc., and its predecessor, the League of Nations, and finally all the rest – the EU, NATO, the OECD and many more. In this short space I will concentrate mostly on the UN and will deal more briefly with a selection of organisations from the other two categories.

The United Nations Organization was founded in 1946 to take over from the League of Nations as a forum for regulating world affairs and to preserve peace in the aftermath of the Second World War. If it has never quite lived up to the hopes and aspirations of its founders, it is undoubtedly still a major factor in international relations and, more to the point of this work, the producer of an extensive programme of publications. These can be grouped into three: 'documents', being internal working papers normally reproduced from typescript, issued free and produced in small quantities; 'publications' or 'sales publications' which are conventionally printed, priced and available for purchase; and, intermediate between the two, though essentially documents, 'official records'. It might be thought that only publications, so-called, need be considered as official publications of the UN, and the rest, the documents and official records, are best considered as archives. The reason the latter are also considered as official publications is that they are included in the material supplied to the extensive network of depository libraries, at least one in each member state, and that these libraries are under an obligation to make their depository collections generally available to the public in their own country. Moreover documents are included in the various guides and indexes to the published output of the UN and, indeed, constitute the bulk of that output.

The documents consist of the reports and papers of the various committees, conferences, councils, commissions, working groups, etc., by which the permanent organs of the UN operate. Each document is identified by an alpha-numeric code called its document number and the prefix to this number (all but the final element) is called the Document Series Symbol. The first element of the code is a letter identifying the organ followed by a letter and number indicating the type of subordinate body and the body itself, followed by a letter indicating the type of document and ending with the number of the document itself. Each element is followed by a slash and not every element is present in each document number (it has to be added that there are variations on this pattern). Few of these documents will have covers and the document number will normally appear at the top of what passes for a title-page. Thus E/CONF.41/1 indicates the first paper delivered to the 2nd World Population Conference, Belgrade, 1965 (being the 41st conference) of the Economic and Social Council. The other principal Organs of the UN are the General Assembly, the Security Council, the Secretariat, and (until 1994 when it was wound up) the Trusteeship Council. Other organs are less obviously dependent on the UN and have been confused with agencies (see below). UNICEF (the UN Children's Fund), the UN Development Programme (UNDP), the Office of the UN High Commissioner for Refugees (UNHCR) and especially the International Court of Justice (ICJ) are examples of these.

The official records of the UN consist of the records of the main organs mentioned above and the ICJ – the records of the plenary sessions of these organs (their '*Hansards*'), documents submitted to them (their 'parliamentary papers'), their Resolutions (the General Assembly and Security Council resolutions are particularly important documents), their budgets, financial reports, decisions, etc., and for the ICJ, its pleadings, judgements, advisory opinions and orders. It should be mentioned that the annual report on the activities of the ICJ is issued as a supplement to the *Official records of the General Assembly* (currently Supplement No.4, formerly No.5). Where appropriate, records are issued in provisional form as separates, during the course of the session and in a consolidated permanent form at the end of the session.

Documents that are anticipated to have a wider appeal and many commissioned studies are produced in a better quality format and are put on sale and these constitute the sales publications. A few of these may carry a document number as described above but this is rare. Instead they will all carry a sales publication number on the back of the title-page. This also is alpha-numeric but, apart from appearing in a different place on the document, the code follows a different sort of pattern (less obviously mnemonic) and the elements are separated by full stops and not slashes. Thus *Aspects of exchange rate determination* is coded E.95.II.F.26.

There are a number of guides to the UN, several produced by itself. *Basic facts about the United Nations* and *Everyone's United Nations* both give a good introduction and include the UN agencies in their coverage and the *Yearbook of the United Nations* gives an annual conspectus of UN activity. Osmanczyk

(Edmund J.) *The encyclopedia of the United Nations*. 3rd ed. New York : Routledge, 2003 contains the texts of important conventions and a few bibliographic references and Baratta (Joseph Preston) *The United Nations system*. Oxford : Clio Press, 1995 (International Organizations series, 10 – others in this series cover the European Communities, Comecon, the Commonwealth, the Organization of African Unity (OAU) and NATO) is a thorough bibliographic guide. A guide to sources is the *Directory of United Nations information sources*, 5th ed. New York : UN, 1994 (GV.E.94.O.14). Peter I. Hajnal has produced two guides to the documentation of the UN: *Directory of United Nations documentary and archival sources*. New York : UN, 1991 and *Guide to United Nations organization, documentation and publishing for students*. Dobbs Ferry, NY : Oceana, 1978. Somewhat different is *The United Nations system and its predecessors*, 2 vols. London : OUP, 1997, which gives the texts for the authorisation of the establishment of the United Nations, its organs and departments, the specialised agencies (see below), the League of Nations and those agencies that predate the UN and have subsequently been assimilated into the UN system. A useful free pamphlet issued by the British Library's Social Sciences and Official Publications department is *United Nations documentation*, in the 'How to find official publications in the British Library's Official Publications and Social Services Reading Area' series. A very useful and frequently updated guide, *United Nations documentation : research guide* produced by the United Nations Dag Hammarskjöld Library is available on the UN website at **http://www.un.org/Depts/dhl/resguide/**

The main current printed index to UN documents is UNDOC (*United Nations documents*) which, with its predecessors, UNDEX (1970–79) and UNDI (1950–73), goes back to 1950. The data contained in these are gradually being added to an online database starting with the present and working backwards (see Chapter 8 for details and for electronic index tools). A somewhat different index is *United Nations document series symbols* which does not index documents but the series symbols by which the documents are identified. The *Complete reference guide to United Nations sales publications 1946–78*, compiled by Mary Eva Birchfield. Pleasantville, NY : Unifo, 1982 is produced in 2 vols., the first volume is 'catalogue' the second 'indexes'. *Series catalogue*. Geneva : UN Library, 1998 is a library catalogue and contains non-UN as well as UN series. The Dag Hammarskjöld Library produces three series of indexes to UN proceedings: *Index to the Proceedings of the General Assembly* (ST/LIB/SER.B/A.1-), *Index to the Proceedings of the Security Council* ST/LIB/SER.B/S.1-) and *Index to the Proceedings of the Economic and Social Council* (ST/LIB/SER.B/E.1-). Some of the organs of the UN have their own indexes such as *UNCTAD 1963–1983 : bibliography*. Geneva, 1983.

Certain key documents have been reprinted in collected commercial editions such as Dusan J. Djonovich's *United Nations. Series I Resolutions adopted by the*

General Assembly 1946–85. Dobbs Ferry, NY : Oceana, 1972–88, 24 vols. and his … *Series II Resolutions and decisions of the Security Council, 1946–79.* Dobbs Ferry, NY : Oceana, 1988–92, 11 vols. Later resolutions are best found through electronic sources (see Chapter 8) where even the bibliographic databases usually include the full texts of resolutions.

So far we have only considered the United Nations itself but this is paralleled by some two dozen 'UN agencies' or 'specialised agencies'. Unlike UNICEF, UNCTAD and the ICJ which are organs of the UN, these are separate organisations even though some have 'United Nations' in their name (e.g. the United Nations Educational, Scientific and Cultural Organization or the Food and Agricultural Organization of the United Nations, more commonly known as Unesco (now adopted as its official name) and the FAO). These organisations are closely related to the UN and largely have a common membership and most have been formed by UN action but some predate the UN and have been subsequently 'adopted' by the UN system. Such is the case with the ILO, the International Labour Organization.

Other agencies include the International Atomic Energy Agency (IAEA), the World Health Organization (WHO), the Universal Postal Union (UPU), the World Meteorological Organization (WMO), the World Intellectual Property Organization (WIPO) and the World Bank Group, several inter-related organisations all based in Washington, DC including the World Bank itself (the International Bank for Reconstruction and Development – IBRD), the International Monetary Fund (IMF) and the International Finance Corporation (IFC). A recent addition to the agencies is the World Trade Organization (WTO) which in 1994 replaced GATT (the General Agreement on Tariffs and Trade) which was always supposed to be an interim organisation. The published output of these agencies varies in quantity but follows the UN pattern. They make the same distinction between documents and (sales) publications and they identify documents by alpha-numeric codes. This practice, in fact, is common to all IGOs and most NGOs as well. Most specialised agencies operate depository systems similar to, though seldom as extensive as, the UN. Sales publications, which are generally outside the depository system, are particularly important for Unesco. Many learned studies on the art and culture of member states have been produced, often in collaboration with commercial publishers. Each agency is responsible for its own catalogue and indexes such as *FAO documentation : current bibliography*. Rome : FAO, monthly, or *Unesco list of documents and publications*. Paris : Unesco, annual with cumulations. There are a number of guides to individual agencies such as Hajnal (Peter I.) *Guide to Unesco*. Dobbs Ferry, NY : Oceana, 1991.

The League of Nations was the predecessor of the United Nations and lasted from 1919 to 1946. A good fairly recent guide is Northedge (F. S.) *The League of Nations : its life and times, 1920–1946*. Leicester : Leicester Univ. Press, 1986. More specifically concerned with the publications of the League is Aufricht (Hans) *Guide to League of Nations publications*. New York : Columbia Univ. Press, 1951. There are two useful catalogues to these publications besides the contemporary indexes of the League now hard to come by, namely the Carnegie Endowment for International Peace's *A repertoire of League of Nations serial documents, 1919–1947*, 2 vols. Dobbs Ferry, NY : Oceana, 1973 and *League of Nations documents, 1919–1946 : a descriptive guide and key to the Microfilm Collection*, 3 vols. New Haven, CT : Research Publications, 1973. This has the advantage in that it is the index to a specific collection, Research Publication's set of League documents on film, but the guide is difficult to use without a good idea of how the League organised its published output.

Beyond the UN system there are a wide range of IGOs. One, however, has had a particular importance in Britain, namely the European Union (the EU). This began when six members joined together to form the European Coal and Steel Community (the ECSC) in 1953. Four years later two new Communities were formed by the same six countries in the Treaties of Rome – the European Atomic Energy Community (Euratom) and the European Economic Community (the EEC, often called the Common Market) and collectively they became known as the European Communities, now renamed the European Union (the EU). Britain joined in 1973 and there are currently 15 members, shortly to rise to 25. The EU is an anomalous IGO in that it has aspirations to become a sovereign entity, the centre of a confederation, or perhaps something even more (the 'ever closer union' of the founding treaties) and its pattern of official publications reflects this. It should be mentioned that all IGOs have an element of sovereignty insofar as the contracting parties agree by binding treaty to abide by the IGO's decisions in matters defined in the relevant treaty. Nevertheless the EU is more state-like than other IGOs. It has its own government gazette, the *Official journal*, its own extensive repertoire of legislation, primary and secondary, and its set of parliamentary debates. The EU issues most of its documents in each of its official languages, either in a single multilingual text or, more usually, in separate language editions. English has been an official language since the accession of Britain and Ireland in 1973 and earlier texts, if still relevant, were translated at that time. English titles only will be quoted below.

The *Official journal of the European Communities* (OJ) is issued daily in three series. The 'L' series (Legislation) contains treaties, regulations, directives, decisions, opinions, recommendations, protocols, resolutions and rules of procedure; the 'C' series (Information and Notices – the initial comes from the French text, 'communications') contains draft laws, job vacancies, resolutions of the Council of

Ministers, minutes, resolutions and written questions of the European Parliament, lists of actions, orders and judgements of the Court of Justice, etc.; the 'S' series (Supplement) contains notices concerning tenders for public works or supply contracts. Part of the 'C' series is only available on CD-ROM or online while the 'S' series ceased to be published in paper form in 1998 and is also now available only electronically (see Chapter 8). In addition, the *Debates of the European Parliament* which contained the debates and oral questions were published as an annex to the OJ 'C' series until 1999, but again are now only available electronically. Finally there is the *Index to the Official journal*, monthly and annual. This in fact only indexes the 'L' series and a small part of the 'C' series concerned with the Court of Justice and is in two parts, a methodological index listing legislative acts and cases by their OJ reference, and an alphabetical index.

An up-to-date guide to the EU is *The European Union handbook*. 2nd ed., edited by Jackie Gower. London : Fitzroy Dearborn, 2002. A guide to EU publications is Ian Thomson's *The documentation of the European Communities : a guide*. London : Mansell, 1989. This is an excellent guide though in need of updating. A good current awareness guide issued bi-monthly by Chadwyck-Healey in association with the Representation of the European Commission in the UK was *European access* (1980–2002), but its closure has left electronic sources as the only option for those seeking this type of information (see Chapter 8). The Office of Official Publications in Luxembourg no longer issues an annual *Catalogue* in paper form, the last being *General catalogue of publications 2001* Luxembourg : EUR-OP, 2001; this is still a useful cumulation of all EU publications from 1985 that remained in print to that date. An annual *Key publications of the European Union* (2000–) is still published.

An important category of EU documentation are COM-Docs (documents of the European Commission) which include early drafts of legislation (later drafts will appear in OJ 'C' series), policy documents, reports on the implementation of policy, and documents of public interest. Originally they were internal documents and not publicly available but although a few remain confidential, most are now available (identified as 'Final'); they are coded: COM (year) number- final, e.g. COM(87) 376 final. COM-Docs can be found on the EUR-lex portal to European law (see Chapter 8).

The OECD (Organization for Economic Co-operation and Development) is an important IGO and, from the point of view of its published output, different from those considered so far in that it consists primarily of publications, that is sales publication, rather than documents. The OECD was founded in 1961, superseding the OEEC (the Organization for European Economic Co-operation) established in 1948 as a part of the Marshall Plan for the economic recovery of war-torn Western Europe. It has been described as 'a club of like-minded countries', that is of the principal developed capitalist countries, 29 at present, comprising the United States, Canada and Mexico in North America, Australia and New Zealand in Oceania, Japan and South Korea in the Far East, and the rest in Europe including the Czech Republic, Hungary and Poland, former members of Comecon, founded by the Soviet Union in opposition to the OEEC and now defunct. It aims to promote policies designed to achieve sustained economic growth and employment and a rising standard of living in member states.

It publishes *News from the OECD* each month, the *OECD Observer* six times a year and the *OECD economic outlook* half-yearly; it publishes a wide range of one-off and serial studies and surveys on a wide range of topics, not all of them obviously economic, for example *Education at a glance : OECD indicators*. But it is best known for its annual economic surveys of individual countries. These began in 1952 as *Surveys of economic conditions in member countries of the OEEC, Canada and the USA* and are now known as *OECD economic surveys [country]*. These cover all member countries and a select few non-member countries and there is now a survey on the Euro Area (in addition to surveys on each of the countries which comprise it). English and French are the only official languages of the OECD and most publications are issued in separate editions for each of them but statistical publications tend to be issued in a single bilingual edition. TSO and formerly HMSO are agents in the UK for OECD and formerly OEEC publications and these will be listed in the TSO *Daily list* and *Monthly catalogue* and in TSO's annual *Agency catalogue*. For current publications, online searching is probably the best (see Chapter 8).

Chapter 8.   Electronic sources

For over five centuries British official publications have been issued in print form and for the most part this continues and is likely to do so for the foreseeable future. But in parallel with this, and sometimes instead of it, publications are now being issued in electronic form, either as CD-ROMs or increasingly in an online format accessible through the Internet. We have seen how each of the devolved governments have used online publishing as the main form of output for most of their publications and that, for the National Assembly for Wales, it is the only form of publication. Increasingly, the same is true of the British government. What is true for full-text publishing is even truer for published guides, indexes and catalogues. As governments and IGOs are using the Internet as a means of disseminating information and as a tool for connecting with a wider public (and sometimes as a way to save money), so they are increasingly making their publications freely available online. The US government has led the way with an astonishing amount of material being released, but in the UK more official publications are now becoming available online as a matter of course. There is a stated intention, for example, to publish all Command Papers online as well as in print, though at the moment this is happening for only around two-thirds of the papers.

This chapter aims to list the principal electronic sources for British and, to a lesser extent, foreign and international official publications both as online sources and, in some cases as CD-ROMs. It makes no pretence to being comprehensive and, given the rapid development in this field, it can only be a snapshot in time. Indeed one of the inherent advantages of online sources over print is the ability to update the data continuously. This does not mean that such data *is* constantly updated. When visiting a site that you are not familiar with, two things are worth checking – the date of the latest update and the number of visits the site has received. The first gives an indication of how up to date a site is and the second how popular it is. Neither is an infallible indicator of the worth of the site. An update may be well short of a thorough revision and popularity may be a poor indication of quality; common sense should be used in evaluating these matters. In particular the number of visits will be influenced by how long the site has been available and by the popularity of the subject matter of the site.

What follows is essentially a list of databases, with firstly a few of the key resources and thereafter arranged broadly in the sequence of the earlier chapters of this work. In each category gateways are noted first followed by a list of selected sites. Some of them are essentially bibliographic databases, that is they list publications but, in general, do not provide the full text of the documents. However, this is now being done selectively or else hot-links are being provided to other databases that do have the documents full text. Other databases are full-text and are sources providing access to the document only in the sense that electronic documents are fully searchable so that you can find a relevant document and then read it. There is another kind of database, an information database, where there is no print equivalent and the database consists of raw data that can be manipulated by the user. These are usually, though not always, statistical databases which one can search and derive information from, tailor-made for the enquirer.

Unless stated otherwise the databases listed are freely available on the Internet. Those that are **subscription services** are available in the Social Sciences Reading Room at the British Library.

Key Resources

- **Ukonline –** This citizen's portal offers access to government information and services online. Information is organised around **your life** such as having a baby, dealing with crime, going away or moving home. **Quick Find** offers a route to sources of government information online through an alphabetical list of agencies and the UltraSeek search engine. It also promises to provide links to official documents which will be invaluable when developed. **CitizenSpace** is intended to make it easier for you to take an active part in the government's decision-making processes. It gives you information you will find useful when exercising your rights as a citizen and enables you to participate in the formulation of policy and law by taking part in current consultation exercises.
  http://www.ukonline.gov.uk/

- **UKOP Online –** The official catalogue of UK official publications. Combines the catalogue of The Stationery Office (TSO) with Chadwyck-Healey's *Catalogue of official publications not published by The Stationery Office*. Coverage is from 1980. Essentially a bibliographic database though it is now increasingly adding to its archive of full-text documents at a rate of around 12,000 items a year. UKOP also creates digitized versions of around 3,000 documents a year where no online versions exist. The full-text archive consists of pdf files so is not dependent on government departments maintaining sites or links.
  This is a subscription service.
  http://www.ukop.co.uk/

- **HMSO Legislation –** Contains the full text of *Public general acts and General Synod measures* from 1988, *Statutory instruments* from 1987, *Northern Irish statutory rules* from 1991, *Acts of the Scottish Parliament*, *Scottish statutory*

instruments and *Statutory instruments* made by the National Assembly for Wales from 1999, *Acts of the Northern Ireland Assembly* from 2000; also draft SIs from 1997, draft SRs from 2000 and draft SSIs from 2001 and the updated *Statutes of Northern Ireland, 1921–2001*; also the *Chronological table of local acts 1797–* and the *Chronological table of private and personal acts 1539–* . N.B. This is legislation as passed; for current law refer to one of the subscription services such as Butterworths (see below).
http://www.hmso.gov.uk/legislation/about_legislation.htm

- **U.K. Parliament** – A general database for parliament with several sections with full text publications: bills (public and private bills before either House in the current Parliament), *Hansard* (bound set of House of Commons' *Debates* from Vol.142 (6th ser.) Sess.1988–89, House of Lords' *Debates* from Vol. 559 (5th Ser.) Sess.1994–95, *Standing Committee debates* from Sess.1998–99, and the current daily Hansards and indexes for both Houses), the 'Vote bundle' for the current day and preceding week, *Standing orders*, selected recent House of Commons papers, the *Weekly information bulletin* from No. 33 of 1995–96 (19 Oct. 1996) and the *Sessional information digest* from Sess.1995–96. Site also has the House of Commons Information Office Factsheet series.
http://www.parliament.uk/

- **National Statistics Online** – Office for National Statistics. This is the official UK statistics site. It is organised around 12 themes, each reflecting a major area of national life, e.g. the economy. It also offers access to full text of 2001 census data, neighbourhood statistics data, and a number of ONS products such as *Population trends*, *Focus on London*, *Labour market trends*, *Social trends*, etc. ONS has published a *National statistics code of practice*. If the code is followed government statistics carry a National Statistics logo which one can see on the data available on a number of departmental websites.
http://www.statistics.gov.uk/

- **Governments on the WWW** – This database includes links to parliaments, executive agencies, law courts, embassies and consulates, and political parties.
http://www.gksoft.com/govt/en/

UK Law

- **Lawlinks KLS** – Annotated list of websites compiled by the Law Library of the University of Kent at Canterbury.
http://library.kent.ac.uk/library/lawlinks/default.htm

- **InfoLaw** – Gateway to UK legal resources on the web. It includes a subscription-based Lawfinder Service.
  http://www.infolaw.co.uk

- **Access to Law** – Legal resources selected and annotated by Inner Temple Library
  http://www.accesstolaw.com/site/

- **Legal Resources for Lawyers** – An independent guide to UK legal resources on the web maintained by Delia Venables.
  http://www.venables.co.uk/sites.htm

- **BAILII** – British and Irish Legal Information Institute. Compilation of British and Irish legislation and case law in full text.
  http://www.bailii.org/

- **House of Lords Judgements** – Full text of all opinions delivered since November 1996.
  http://www.publications.parliament.uk/pa/ld199697/ldjudgmt/ldjudgmt.htm

- **Butterworth's Direct** – Gives access to various Butterworth's databases including Halsbury's Law Direct, Legislation Direct, Human Rights Direct and All England Direct databases.
  This is a subscription service.
  http://www.butterworths.com/butterworths.asp

- **Current Legal Information Online** – A fully searchable source of reference to case law, statutes, statutory instruments, legal articles and grey literature in field.
  This is a subscription service.
  http://193.118.187.160/cli.htm

- **LexisNexis Professional** – Comprehensive full-text database covering statutes, statutory instruments, English case law since 1936, and selected UK law journals.
  This is a subscription service.
  http://www.lexis-nexis.com/pro

- **Justis.com** – Gives access to various databases such as Statute Law (current UK statutes from 1235 with cross-references between amending and amended legislation), Electronic Law Reports (as produced by the Incorporated Council of Law Reporting) from 1865 to date, etc.
  This is a subscription service.
  http://www.justis.com

- **Tribunals Homepage** – Gives links to the websites of the Social Security and Child Support Commissioners, Immigration Appellate Authority, Special Commissioners of Income Tax, VAT and Duties Tribunal and Lands Tribunal, which include full text of selected decisions.
  http://www.courtservice.gov.uk/tribunals/index.htm

UK Parliament

- **Early Day Motions** – A House of Commons Library database containing full-text EDMs from 1997–98 Session.
  http://edm.ais.co.uk

- **BOPCRIS (British Official Publications Collaborative Reader Information Service)** – Bibliographic database for official publications covering 1688–1995. The material covered is primarily UK Parliamentary Papers and includes digitized full-text of a limited number of documents.
  http://www.bopcris.ac.uk

- **Index to HC Papers, 1801–** – Cumulative index to House of Commons papers, House of Commons bills and Command papers. Session 1801–1994/95.
  This is a subscription CD-ROM.

- **Official-Documents.co.uk** – The Stationery Office. Full-text archive of a selection of parliamentary papers dating from 1994.
  http://www.official-documents.co.uk/

- **History of Parliament** – History of Parliament Trust. Contains the revised text of all seven of the sets of *History of Parliament* published up to 1998 (1386–1421, 1509–1558, 1558–1603, 1660–1690, 1715–1754, 1754–1790, 1790–1820)
  This is a subscription CD-ROM. For information, see:
  http://www.histparl.ac.uk

- **POLIS** – Parliamentary Online Indexing Service. Indexes the proceedings and publications of both Houses of Parliament at Westminster from 1997. Maintained and updated by House of Commons Library.
  http://www.polis.parliament.uk

- **Parlianet** – Index to the proceedings and publications of both Houses of Parliament at Westminster from 1979. It also includes material from the National Assembly for Wales and the Northern Ireland Assembly. Provides links to full-text documents.
  This is a subscription service.
  http://www.parlianet.com

Other UK sites

- **Social Science Information Gateway (SOSIG)** – This is the leading online catalogue of high quality Internet resources aimed at researchers and practitioners in the social sciences, business and law. All resources are selected, evaluated and described by experts. The catalogue can be browsed or searched by subject.
  http://www.sosig.ac.uk/

- **Tagish** – Comprehensive alphabetical lists of UK local authority and other local government related websites.
  http://www.tagish.co.uk/local/

- **Police Services of the UK** – Official list of police forces and police related organisations.
  http://www.police.uk/

- **UK Criminal Justice Web Links** – University of Leeds, Department of Law. List focuses on criminal justice sites relating to the United Kingdom, with more selective links for Continental Europe, North America and the rest of the world.
  http://www.leeds.ac.uk/law/ccjs/ukweb.htm

- **King's Fund** – Maintains a comprehensive set of links covering NHS and UK government sites, policy and research organisations and subject specific sites in fields arranged alphabetically under broad subject headings.
  http://www.kingsfund.org.uk/Library/Links.cfm

- **The Stationery Office** – The official website of the Stationery Office Ltd. It contains the *Daily lists* from the beginning of 2000 but its main bibliographic database is **UKOP Online** (see above).
  http://www.tso.co.uk/

- **Inforoute** – A developing gateway to the information held by UK government departments in the shape of databases, paper files, statistics collections, research reports, etc. It is based on the Government's Information Asset Register which is an amalgamation of the Asset Registers being compiled by each government department, agency and quango. A potentially very useful site accessing otherwise *unpublished* government information. Site still under construction.
  http://www.inforoute.hmso.gov.uk/

- **DfES Statistics** – Department for Education and Skills. Site provides a single gateway to statistical data on education, training and life-long learning and skills produced by the DfES and includes staff contacts for more information.
  http://www.dfes.gov.uk/statistics/

- **Audit Commission** – Includes local authority performance indicators.
  http://www.audit-commission.gov.uk/

- **Defence Analytical Services Agency** – Links to downloadable version of some statistical products, including web edition of *UK defence statistics*, the annual statistical compendium of the Ministry of Defence.
  http://www.dasa.mod.uk/

- **Department of Health** – Provides access to statistical press releases, reports on Department of Health surveys and statistical returns and tables available on the Internet, and to a full list of publications. Includes *HPSSS* (*Health and Personal Social Services Statistics*), an overview of statistics from the Department of Health.
  http://www.doh.gov.uk/public/stats1.htm

- **Department for Work and Pensions. Information and Analysis Directorate** – Contains statistics on families and children, working age, pensions, and family resources, with sections on summary statistics and other statistics, mostly on benefits.
  http://www.dwp.gov.uk/asd/index.asp

- **Department for Transport** – Follow the 'Transport Statistics' link on the departmental home page to access a range of statistical data.
  http://www.dft.gov.uk

- **Office of the Deputy Prime Minister** – For statistical data on housing, homelessness and planning, follow the links from the 'What we do' menu.
  http://www.odpm.gov.uk/

- **Higher Education Funding Council for England** – Follow the link to 'publications' to access full-text HEFCE reports, including those containing statistical data such as performance indicators in higher education.
  http://www.hefce.ac.uk/Pubs/

- **Higher Education Statistics Agency** – Site contains a publications list and details of their priced enquiry service, but also a 'Free online statistics section' that includes data on disability, ethnicity, etc.
  http://www.hesa.ac.uk/

- **Department for Environment, Food and Rural Affairs, Economics and Statistics** – Produces a wide range of statistics covering much of the agriculture, fisheries and food industries. All main releases of statistics are shown on this site in the form of pdf files and many detailed statistics are made available in spreadsheet format.
  http://www.defra.gov.uk/esg/

- **The National Archives** – Formed in 2003; brings together the Public Record Office and the Historical Manuscripts Commission. **http://www.nationalarchives.gov.uk/**

- **1901 Census** – Access to the online index of the census returns for 1901 is free but access to the returns themselves is **subscription based**. **http://www.pro.gov.uk/online/census.htm**

- **Foreign & Commonwealth Office** – For the FCO's Treaty Section go to 'Official Documents' under the 'Directory and Documents' menu. **http://www.fco.gov.uk/**

- **UK-Info Disk** – UK electoral roll on CD-ROM (issued annually; also available online as **www.192.com**). **This is a subscription CD-ROM.**

- **Gazettes Online** – Contains the *London gazette* online from Jan. 1998 and, in an archive section (to be expanded), all the issues containing honours and awards from the beginning of the twentieth century and all the issues for the periods of both World Wars. Access also to the *Edinburgh gazette* and the *Belfast gazette*. **http://www.gazettes-online.co.uk**

- **Scottish Parliament** – Includes Parliamentary debates, reports of committees, business papers, bills, etc. **http://www.scottish-parliament.uk/**

- **Scottish Executive** – Formerly the Scottish Office. Details the changes in its functions since the creation of the Scottish Parliament and includes the full text of most Scottish Executive documents since 1998. **http://www.scotland.gov.uk/**

- **Northern Ireland Assembly** – Includes election results, Parliamentary debates, committee reports, Assembly reports, etc. **http://www.ni-assembly.gov.uk**

- **Northern Ireland Executive** – For information on the administration of government in Northern Ireland. **http://www.northernireland.gov.uk**

- **National Assembly for Wales** – All the publications of the Assembly are available via its website, which, for most categories, is the only form of publication, so includes statistics, annual reports, circulars and consultation papers, as well as the expected Assembly papers. **http://www.wales.gov.uk/index.htm**

- **Office of the Deputy Prime Minister – Devolution pages**. The ODPM is responsible for the management of relations between the UK government and the devolved administrations, as well as overseeing the proposed introduction of English regional assemblies.
http://www.odpm.gov.uk/stellent/groups/odpm_devolution/documents/sectionhomepage/odpm_devolution_page.hcsp

Foreign Official Publications

- **Parline Database** – Inter-Parliamentary Union. Includes general information on national parliaments worldwide such as a description of the electoral system, results of the most recent elections, information on the presidency of each chamber, information on the mandate and status of members of parliament, and links to the websites of parliaments.
http://www.ipu.org/parline-e/parlinesearch.asp

- **Oultwood** – Links to local authority websites in the UK, Canada, Australia, New Zealand, South Africa and the Republic of Ireland.
http://www.oultwood.com/

- **International Politics Department – University of Aberystwyth** – This page contains a useful collection of links to internet sites covering international relations and security issues.
http://www.aber.ac.uk/interpol/links/index.html

- **Social Security Websites around the World** – Links to social security agencies and organisations worldwide maintained by the US Social Security Administration.
http://www.ssa.gov/international/links.html

- **Social Security Worldwide** – International Social Security Association. Offers five databases providing concise outlines of social security systems in over 170 countries, summaries of reforms since 1995, references to legislation, bibliography of materials on social protection issues and thesaurus of key terms. 1988– (issued twice a year).
This is a subscription CD-ROM.

- **OFFSTATS: Official Statistics on the Web** – Country lists give links to web pages provided by statistical offices, central banks and government departments; the topics list is comprised of links to the statistics pages of inter-governmental organisations.
http://www.auckland.ac.nz/lbr/stats/offstats/OFFSTATSmain.htm

- **Findlaw** – Extensive site with links to worldwide legal information.
http://www.findlaw.com/index.html

- **World Law** – World Legal Information Institute. A global index and search engine for law.
  http://www.worldlii.org/catalog/

- **Eagle-I Service** – Institute of Advanced Legal Studies. Electronic access to global legal information.
  http://www.worldlii.org/catalog/

- **Guide to Law Online** – Law Library of Congress. Annotated hypertext guide to sources of information on government and law worldwide available free via the Internet. For US law the site gives access to full text of *The US Code, Code of federal regulations, Federal register, Statutes at large* (1st–43rd Congress, 1789–1875, including the *Declaration of independence*, the *Articles of confederation*, the *Constitution* plus amendments, and the texts of treaties with Indians and with foreign nations) and *Public laws* (104th Congress, 1st Session, 1995–).
  http://www.loc.gov/law/guide/index.html

- **USGPO-Access** – The official US Government Printing Office's gateway to federal government information. Gives quick links providing direct access to the *Code of federal regulations*, the *Federal register*, the *US Code*, the *Congressional record*, and documents and reports, congressional hearings, GAO reports, weekly compilation of presidential documents, public laws, bills, etc.
  http://www.gpoaccess.gov/index.html

- **FirstGov** – Official website for searching for US government information. Provides links to the executive, legislative and judicial branches of the federal government, a search engine, and facilities for browsing by subject.
  http://www.firstgov.gov/

- **Fedgate** – Independent site run by a non-profit-making body. Links to US federal government departments and agencies arranged by category.
  http://fedgate.org/

- **Fedstat** – The best official site for US government statistics. Provides access to statistical information produced by over 100 US federal government agencies.
  http://www.fedstats.gov/

- **University of Michigan Documents Center** – Excellent resource that gives links to US federal government, foreign governments, international agencies and US state and local governments. For an example see next item.
  http://www.lib.umich.edu/govdocs/

- **Government Gazettes Online** – University of Michigan Documents Center. Links to the websites of official gazettes worldwide.
  http://www.lib.umich.edu/govdocs/gazettes/index.htm

- **International Constitutional Law** – Wuerzberg University. Constitutional documents and country information.
  http://www.oefre.unibe.ch/law/icl/index.html

- **A–Z World Constitutions** – Charter 88. Links to national and international constitutions.
  http://www.charter88.org.uk/links/link_cons.html

- **International Census Collection** – University of Texas at Austin. For bibliographic information on census publications.
  http://www.dev.lib.utexas.edu/pcl/icc/

- **Social Policy Virtual Library** – International Social and Public Policy Research Information Gateway. Provides links to sites of major organisations, research institutes, libraries, journals, online databases and data sources, mailing lists and discussion groups in field.
  http://www.social-policy.org

- **Thomas** – Full text of US legislation (bills and public laws) and the *Congressional record*, and links to congressional committee information.
  http://thomas.loc.gov/

- **LLRX.com Resource Center – International Law Guides** – Guides to the legal systems of a range of countries, and Internet resources available. Good starting point for online research into legal system of a particular country.
  http://www.llrx.com/comparative_and_foreign_law.html

- **GPO on SilverPlatter** – Online version of the US Government Printing Office *Monthly catalog*, offering bibliographic records of US government publications from July 1976 to the present.
  This is a subscription service.
  http://www.silverplatter.com/

- **Statistical abstract of the United States** – Web versions of the annual compilation of social and economic statistics in full text from 1995.
  http://www.census.gov/statab/www/

- **United States. Bureau of the Census. International Data Base** – Databank of demographic and socio-economic statistical tables for 227 countries.
  http://www.census.gov/ipc/www/idbnew.html

Inter-Governmental Organisations

- **United Nations** – Access to the UN's free Internet site. The gateway to all UN sites.
  http://www.un.org/

- **Access UN** – Web-based Index to United Nations Documents and Publications, with links to full text of documents when available free on the Internet.
  This is a subscription service.
  http://infoweb.newsbank.com

- **Official Documents System of the United Nations** – Provides access to the full text of United Nations documentation and official records from 1992 and resolutions from 1946 to the present.
  This is a subscription service.
  http://www.ods.un.org/ods/

- **Dag Hammarskjold Library, UN Bibliographic Information System (UNBISnet)** – Catalogue of UN publications and documents from 1979 and non-UN publications held in the collections of the Dag Hammarskjold Library. Intended to act as the gateway to the UN Official Documents System (see above).
  http://unbisnet.un.org/

- **United Nations Treaty Collection** – Full text collection of treaties and international agreements registered or filed and recorded with and published by the UN Secretariat since 1946.
  This is a subscription service.
  http://untreaty.un.org/

- **UN Press Release Database** – UN press releases from 1995 onwards with keyword and fielded search facilities.
  http://www.un.org/News/

- **UN Office of the High Commissioner for Human Rights** – Full text of treaties relating to human rights and documents issued by both the charter-based and treaty-based bodies.
  http://www.unhchr.ch/

- **International Law** – United Nations site giving access to the International Criminal Court, the International Court of Justice, and the Criminal Tribunals for former Yugoslavia and for Rwanda.
  http://www.un.org/law/

- **European Union** – Access to Europa, the main server of the European Union, which provides links to the home pages of the Commission, the European Parliament, European Court, Eurostat, etc.
  http://europa.eu.int/

- **EUR-OP** – The Publications Office of the European Union.
  http://eur-op.eu.int/general/en/index_en.htm

- **European Commission Library Catalogue** – Catalogue contains over 172,000 bibliographic records for books, journal articles, conference proceedings and Internet resources. Searches can be conducted in English or French.
  http://europa.eu.int/eclas/

- **KnowEurope** – Information about the institutions, structures, countries, regions, peoples, policies and processes of the EU and wider Europe.
  This is a subscription service.
  http://www.knoweurope.net/

- **Eur-Lex** – The European Union legal portal gives free access to the *Official journal* 'L' and 'C' Series in full text from 1998, links to full text of legislation, treaties and case law and a directory of EU legislation in force. Includes links to case-law since 1997, competition law, the Court of the European Free Trade Association (EFTA) and the European Court of Human Rights.
  http://europa.eu.int/eur-lex/en/index.html

- **Eurolaw** – Covers in full text all the treaties of the EU; the directives and regulations; proposed legislation; case law; national implementation details; parliamentary questions and information and notices from the 'C' series of the *Official journal.*
  This is a subscription service.
  http://www.ili.co.uk/

- **European Court of Justice** – Full text of case law from mid-1997.
  http://curia.eu.int/en/index.htm

- **Legislative Observatory** – European Parliament site giving legislative histories.
  http://wwwdb.europarl.eu.int/dors/oeil/en/default.htm

- **RAPID** – Press and Communication Services of the European Commission. Database of press releases of most EU institutions.
  http://europa.eu.int/rapid/start/welcome.htm

- **International Labour Organization** – Free access to a range of databases covering labour administration, labour legislation, labour statistics, vocational training and country information.
  http://www.ilo.org/

- **International Monetary Fund** – Free site offering access to background information on the IMF and its relations with nation states and full text of selected publications in the *Working papers and Staff country report* series, current and past edition of the *World economic outlook*, etc.
  http://www.imf.org/

- **OECD** – Organisation for Economic Co-operation and Development website.
  http://www.oecd.org/

- **SourceOECD** – Organisation for Economic Co-operation and Development. Provides online access to OECD publications. **This is a subscription service.**
  http://www.oecd.org/

- **Organization for Security and Co-operation in Europe (OSCE)** – Provides a description of OSCE's structure and field activities and access to a virtual library containing documents, journals and decisions issued by various OSCE negotiating bodies from 1973 to the present.
  http://www.osce.org.

- **Pan American Health Organization** – Offers country health profiles, full text of technical documents and access to a range of relevant databases.
  http://www.paho.org/default.htm

- **Unesco** – Access to full-text Executive Board and General Conference documents from 1995 and resolutions and decisions since 1946. Also features a bibliographic database covering Unesco documents and sales publications and a range of statistical data.
  http://www.unesco.org/

- **World Bank Group** – Information on the Bank's research, policies and programmes in areas ranging from pensions to climate change, including many full-text documents. Includes statistical information drawn from the *World Development Indicators*. The Group includes the IBRD, IDA, IFC, MIGA, and ICSID.
  http://www.worldbank.org/

- **World Health Organization** – Information on the WHO's programmes, plus factual information on a range of diseases and their control. Gives access to WHOLIS, the WHO library database which indexes the organisation's own publications, and WHOSIS, the WHO Statistical Information System.
  http://www.who.int/

Appendix

DEFINITION OF OFFICIAL PUBLICATIONS FOR INTERNATIONAL USE

by

International Federation of Library Associations and Institutions
Official Publications Section

Adopted August 1983

After three years of discussion, the IFLA Official Publications Section has adopted a definition of official publications for use internationally – for instance in library schools, in the design of courses, in international exchange, within libraries, or in the arrangement of bibliographies. It is an attempt – brave, some will say – to provide a working guide that will be useful everywhere, while accommodating the profound differences of interpretation that exist even between countries that are geographically and culturally close.

Definition

1. An official publication is any item produced by reprographic or any other method, issued by an organisation that is an official body, and available to an audience wider than that body.

2. An official body is:

   (I)   any legislature of a state, or federation of states; or of a province (state) or regional, local or other administrative sub-division;

   (II) any executive agency of the central government of such a state or federation of states or of a province (state) or regional, local or other administrative sub-division;

   (III) any court or judicial organ;

   (IV) any other organisation which was set up by an official body as in (I), (II) and (III) above, and maintains continuing links with that body whether through direct funding or through its reporting mechanism or its accountability;

(V) any organisation of which the members belong to any of the above 4 categories, including intergovernmental organisations.

provided that the body is considered to be official in the country concerned.

3. An official publication is defined by the status of the issuing source regardless of the subject-matter, content or physical form.

Notes

(1) For the purposes of this definition, the term "official publication" is comparable to terms used in some countries, such as "government publication" and "government document".

(2) The following bodies:
- universities
- learned societies and academies
- industrial and trade associations and chambers of commerce
- libraries, museums and art galleries
- independent research institutes not direct recipients of public funds
will be included as official bodies according to the practice of the individual country.

(3) Political parties will not normally be considered as official bodies unless in the practice or constitution of a particular country there is reason to do so.

(4) Nationalised enterprises and banks, public corporations and other statutory bodies set up to carry out industrial or other productive activity will be considered as official bodies according to the practice of the individual country. However, state majority ownership of capital and heavy direct subsidy in enterprises that are otherwise nominally independent will not cause those enterprises to be considered as official bodies.

(5) Publications originating in official bodies but published by or with the co-operation of commercial firms, universities or independent research institutes, or any other non-official bodies, will normally be considered as official publications.